REFLECTIONS FROM THE MAN IN THE MIRROR

Timothy A. Natale

Ben,
Build your own
track record.
Enjoy.

Dedication

This book is dedicated to
Chris Doyle and
SGT Kamien Stanford (Stan)
and the men and women who have given
their lives for this country.

I made it home to write this book,
but not everyone did.

Contents

Introduction...5

The Man Who Showed Me the Mirror 11

No! Don't Take the Candy Again 21

The Champ is Down but He's Not Out..................27

The Queen...35

Brothers Fight 39

DOMSQUAD 46

The Mayor 52

Michael, Michael, Motorcycle… 58

The Three Stooges 62

The Bachelor Pad...68

The Squad Leader 74

Good Ol' Gregor 80

Federal Escort 85

Ry Guy 95

SHANEO-V-HAS-TO-PEE 100

Made in America...107

Mr. Minor...114

The Blood of Calhooooon 123

The Little Irish Boy 128

The Little Engine That Could 139

He's Like a Piece of Iron 146

Double Threat 153

Somebody Call Somebody! 162

Mini Me 170

Family Away from Home 178

Acknowledgements...189

The Bridge 194

Introduction

A wise man once told me that I was put on this earth to make an impact in someone's life. It may be just one person, or it may end up being a whole lot more. Early in my life when my father first told me that, I laughed it off like most kids my age would. I just wanted have fun and be cool. I didn't want to think about changing the world because I didn't even know what I was doing the next day, let alone in my future. I had a great childhood, and I wouldn't trade it for the world but it took me a long time to realize just how great it was.

My family was blessed financially, and I had every opportunity a person could dream of provided for me. My father worked a lot, and at a young age, that's all I saw. A child doesn't know how much school costs, or the cars, food, bills; they just know dad's not home much. My father would try to explain it to me when I was younger, but the more he tried the angrier I became. I told him countless times that I didn't want or need the money, but I couldn't have been more wrong.

As I grew older I slowly started to see why he gave us the life we had, because my dad didn't spend his money on himself. In fact, I can honestly say my father's sole purpose in life is to make a difference in the lives of others. As the years went by, I came to realize how many people would give everything they had for the life my father gave me; the opportunities he provided that I was throwing down the drain. He worked a lot yes; but I can't put into words the generosity that runs through his veins. He preached to my brothers and I about "making God smile" and "making a difference" but it took me a really long time to realize he wasn't just a preacher; he was a doer.

My mother taught preschool for a while, and now she is a successful small business owner. My Dad, whom I mentioned, is a very successful attorney, and my two brothers are Dominic and Nicholas. Dominic is my younger brother by three years, and Nicholas is my older brother by two. We live the majority of our life in an incredible house in the Chagrin Falls, Ohio area. My dad's side of the family has lived within 30 minutes of us my entire life. I grew up going to my grandparents for lunch on Sundays, with all nine grandkids there. Aunts and Uncles were the core of the family get togethers. My mother's family lived in southern Ohio near Dayton, and I don't see them nearly as much as I was blessed to when I was younger. From day one, I was raised with family being the backbone of my life and wouldn't want it any other way.

My family had its struggles just like most, but one of our toughest hurdles was with my older brother Nicholas who has spent the majority of his life battling significant mental disabilities. His struggle started as early as I can remember and have led him through countless highs and lows. It has pushed him down and held him in some pretty dark places in his life, but Nick is a survivor and with some help he gets right back on top. When I was young, Nick and I wrote the book on sibling rivalry. When the local Fox news affiliate comes to your house to do a sibling rivalry documentary, you know you're heading down a slippery slope. With Nick's disabilities, it was hard for my little brother Dominic and I to understand what to do or how to act in certain scenarios. Nick has been in and out of both inpatient and outpatient treatment facilities and hospitals. You name it he has been there. I would be lying if I didn't acknowledge that the family found itself separated for a long period of time because of some of these issues, but it wasn't just Nick's fault.

Nick and I share some pretty amazing times these days, and we both have grown up substantially. Nick taught me that we all have good and bad experiences in life, but how we deal with those experiences is what defines us. The people who are a part of those experiences play just as vital of a role. You are your experiences, and the people who you grow up with are what make you the person you are. My dad always used to tell me: "Look at the man in the mirror when you wake up and ask yourself who do you want to be." It took years of hearing that daily to really understand what he meant. He said "who" not "what". He told me I could be anything I want, like most parents tell their kids, but this was different. It wasn't about finding a profession. It was much deeper than that, and it took me a long time to realize exactly what he meant. He wanted me to develop a man in the mirror I could be proud of. To be a man of values, live to make a difference, offer myself up for the benefit of others, lead by example, and be reliable.

Nick continues to struggle, but there is something about Nick that I couldn't be more proud of; he doesn't quit. He has fallen into some very dark places, even recently, but he gets up and jumps right back in the fight and there is nothing I respect more than someone who doesn't quit.

I used to look at myself in the mirror and see anger or frustration. It was overwhelming to look at myself because all I saw was what I assumed was failure. I was an average athlete, my grades were terrible, and my relationships were always jacked up. I felt alone because I couldn't find a way to express this anger. I genuinely hated looking at myself because I didn't respect the man I saw. I battled nightmares, depression and anxiety from my experiences with Nick. I blamed myself for so much of my family struggles that I began to dread that look in the mirror each morning.

Each day when I looked in the mirror I met anger, loneliness, frustration and failure. It wasn't until I took what Nick showed me and gave it some deeper thought that I realized I was looking at the man in the mirror the wrong way.

Could it be that life wasn't just about me? Over the years and up until college, all I ever worried about was myself: I was scraping by from day to day. My grades were terrible; my relationships were slipping, and I would have ended up in a totally different place in life had I not realized how much I had around me. I changed my thinking so that when I looked in the mirror, I could make that person who I wanted him to be. It's never too late to change. I didn't like who I was, but that's the best part; even though you can't erase the past, you can create the future.

With each passing day, the reflection in the mirror started to look a lot more hopeful because I started to envision everyone who was fighting this battle with me. I had all these people right by my side trying to help me become the man they all knew I could be. When I look in the mirror now I don't just see myself, I see the people who taught me to be a man. They taught me to pick myself up, dust myself off, and keep going. So often in our lives, people tell you that you may look like your mom or dad, brother or sister, aunt or uncle etc.; but as I looked around and saw all these people I looked up to, and who helped me back on my feet I realized it was much deeper than just a mere resemblance. I began to take on and try to copy the characteristics and traits that I admired in them, just like a young kid may mimic his favorite sports player. I began doing this with my heroes in my everyday life. How could I ever explain to these people the significance they made in my life? They have no idea that, without them, I may not be here today.

When I was 20 years old, I enlisted in the United States Army. At the time I was enrolled at Kent State University, but I had no grades to show for myself, and I knew it was time for change. My family had given me everything, and up until this point I had thrown 90% of it down the drain. My dad has made a huge impact in this world, even if he doesn't admit it, and as cliché as it may sound I was willing to give my life to ensure he could continue to do so. My biggest fear growing up and to this very day is letting down the people who relied on and believed in me, especially my father. When it came to school and chores, that fear be-came reality more often than not. It was time for me to show everyone exactly how much they meant to me. I wanted to show them that I had enough of living my life in the shadows, and even though I didn't have much to show for myself, this time would be different. I was willing to give my life to show my family that I was done living my life as average. I promised myself I would pour my entire heart and soul into the military - the Army- because it wasn't only my dream as a little boy, but because I only saw two options. Option one: giving my life in protection of the ones I love. Option two: returning home to live my life the way my family and friends intended for me to live. At this point in my life I was willing to accept either option. I made a commitment: I would never take another step backwards, I would only take leaps forward and show everyone that they could count on Tim Natale.

This was only the beginning of being proud of the "man in the mirror" and let me tell you that it's an addictive feeling. I wasn't making millions of dollars, or driving fancy cars, but I had pride in myself and realized it was never too late to turn the tables. It was my turn to begin my legacy, but I knew I could not do it alone. I wish to share with you some of the lessons I've learned from the people I've met so far in my life, and how they have helped me build the man in the mirror.

The Man Who Showed Me the Mirror

For anyone who knows my father, it probably won't catch you by surprise to know that he set the mold for the man I wanted to see in the mirror. He taught me if there is one thing I couldn't live without it was "passion." Whether it was a relationship, mulching the yard, coaching football, or the military, he insisted it couldn't be done without passion. My father is a passionate man, and it sounds crazy to me that I'm admitting this, but his life philosophy couldn't be more dead on. His passion springs from making a positive difference in someone's life, and he is right: there is no better feeling in the world. I couldn't imagine growing up without my father, because he has become one of my greatest friends. Not only did he teach me the importance of passion, but without even realizing it, he showed me that you can't do everything by yourself. Life is the ultimate team sport; even Jesus had his followers who helped him change the world.

Whether it was holding a few nails for him while he built something (he could fix anything), or waking up for 7 a.m. Mass, sleepy but inspired, I seized every chance I could to be next to my dad. He could make me so angry at times, and I used to get so upset with how strict and tough he acted until the day I was truly tested on what type of man I was going to be. It was like muscle memory because, as much as dads may sound like broken records, I started to catch myself telling my friends, fellow soldiers, and even people I barely knew the same life lessons my father told me. It's a beautiful cycle, and I couldn't be happier to be a part of it.

His passion for excellence meant he has a short temper over the smallest things. If I was helping him build a shelf and he said "Go get me that thing over there" without even pointing (he still does this), he would get so frustrated that I brought him the screwdriver instead of the towel he wanted. God forbid I tried to use rational thinking. I just couldn't help but laugh. Who on earth would have guessed while my father is building a shelf in the garage, his saying "go get that thing over there" meant go inside and get him the green rag that is on the washing machine and not a practical tool sitting two feet away. I couldn't get enough though; I was his biggest fan. Despite of all the hours he worked, he was there when I needed him. He was at all my sports games, and no matter how much I screwed up, he was there to show me how to set things right. When I say he showed me how, he didn't give me the answers. As a young kid, I hated that. When we are young, we just want the answers and to move on. That wasn't an option with my dad. He gave me the tools to find the answers so, as my life went on, I could continue to find the answers myself, and help those who were struggling like I was. I knew that there was not a single thing I wanted more from life than to grow up and be even half the man my dad is.

My dad is very successful financially but doesn't show it. Being humble is essential in life. Arrogance can destroy the most talented and hardworking people. We had a big house, and he did own a Porsche at one point, but the license plate to that Porsche was "HRDWORK". There was a lesson in everything my father did, and for a while, I didn't see it. There was a period where my father and I let some of the issues get between us. I was the kid who thought he knew it all, and I pushed my father away for a while when things got bad with my brother Nick. I sold myself short in school, and for that matter, life, up until the day I joined the Army. There was a pivotal point in my relationship with my father that I attribute to making a huge impact on why I enlisted.

I had torn part of my Achilles my freshman year in football, and I missed the majority of the season. I made the choice to end the 4-year high school football career I hoped for, and it wasn't easy. It was tough because my closest friends to this day are the group I met playing football. It was even tougher because my father is the reason I started playing anyway. Football was the one thing my father and I shared that was just ours. My brothers hated it. I was crushed when I thought it ended.

My dad had been the coach of St. Rita's football team since I was in sixth grade and decided to keep coaching after I graduated (he is still the coach there, 14 years later). He saw the sadness that leaving a sport I loved brought me and offered me a job on "his staff." I started to "coach" with my dad just because it meant at least five nights a week I got to spend with him. He wasn't just a coach; this was his passion. Don't get me wrong, he knows the sport, but this was his chance to show these young men who Andy Natale is. He got the chance to teach through football that, when you do anything and you do it with passion, you make yourself and the world better. I was a sophomore in high school and had obviously known my father for 14 years, but I had never seen him like this before.

He was happy on the field and you could see it in his eyes that he knew he could make a difference there. There were always parents who said he yelled too much, or he was too intense, but it wasn't negative....it was pure passion to his core. My father changed kids' lives, and I got to witness this first hand. I got to see what he had been preaching to me my whole life, in action. I got to witness what happens when these kids invested their heart and soul into what he was teaching them. The look in their eyes when they had succeeded was special, but the look in his eyes, when they came back to thank him weeks, months, or even years later, was priceless.

Not all the kids we coached went on to play high school football, but still they would come back to the practice field the next year, send him email, or call him just to tell him how much he impacted their lives. I told him year after year: If you change just one kid's life every year, just one kid truly buys into what your preaching, imagine the impact on the world if he makes that same impact on someone's life down the road. Just imagine what would happen if that started a chain effect all because even one kid saw how much you cared, how passionate you were, how Coach Natale believed in them, you can change the world, Dad. And that's exactly what he did, and continues to do on that same field. These young men and their families adore my father, and rightfully so.

This is when I truly started to open my heart to the calling I felt to join the military. I remember specifically a kid I coached my first year on my dad's staff. His name was

Dane; Dane O'Driscoll. He was an incredible athlete, and he had the size to dominate the league. At that age, kids with athletic ability tend to follow two paths. One being the path of being humble and coachable, the other being like too many athletes whose egos grow to outweigh their talent. Dane made his own path. He was a coach's dream. He would sit in the group when dad was talking like he was learning this all for the first time. He excelled in every aspect of the game, but every single day he would look to my father for guidance. He would knock someone 30 feet, but go help them up. When Dane was in 8th grade he towered over me, but he was the most respectful kid on the field.

Dane went on the play high school football at Walsh Jesuit. Week by week, he would contact my dad. He would ask my dad to come to his games, I even went to a few. He would call my dad and tell him how nervous he was before a game, but how he remembered everything my dad taught him. My father was like a little kid on Christmas when he heard his phone ring and it was Dane. There were even a few times Dane doubted his ability, but with a few words of encouragement Dane drove forward. Dane then went on to play for Duquesne University in Pennsylvania.

Without hesitation, each week my father would receive a call from Dane. It would bring tears to my father's eyes to realize he must have done something right for this man to keep calling him four, five, six, seven, and now eight years after he graduated for not only football, but for life questions and even just to talk.

You should have seen the look in Dane's eyes when he saw my father and I sitting in the bleachers for one of his games. He was enormous, built like a brick house, but as humble as they come. You would catch him glancing over at us before a play, or after he did something great, almost to tell my father "that was for you Coach". People like Dane, I'm convinced, will take what my father taught him and go out and change the world and teach it to others.

I started to realize the world would not be the same without people like my father, Dane, my family, and friends who were actually trying to make a difference in the world. Up until this point, honestly up until the day I sat with Dane and my father at Buffalo Wild Wings and saw the way Dane looked at my father, I had lived my life being average and taking advantage of everything that had been provided for me. I knew it was time for me to show my father what he meant to me; that what he was doing for the world, for people he barely knew, was something this world needed. Years later, Dane graduated from Duquesne and came back to coach with my father and I. It's amazing to see the impact he has had on these young men and their lives that over a decade later they come back to help him coach kids on the same field that it all started for them.

My father had given me everything I could ever imagine, and I couldn't think of any way to repay him and the others who helped me turn my life around. How do you explain to people that their impact on your life, without even realizing what they were doing...kept you alive?

I enlisted in the military because it was time for me to show people like my father that I was willing to give my life to protect what they do for this world. I owed these people everything, because without them I may not be here to even write this book. I failed at the majority of things I started in my life not because I lacked talent, but because I was selfish. I lived for myself and never fully invested my heart and soul into what I was doing. Big or small, my father has told me since I was young that "everything matters". My father stood by my side every single time whether I failed or succeeded. He didn't give me the answers, and I wouldn't be where I am today if he did. He guided me to find them on my own. He gave me every single opportunity a boy could ask for, and at that time, a boy is all I was. My father gave me the tools to become the man I am; he gave me the opportunities to make any life I wanted for myself and the ones I love. He gave me a life people would die for, and I was willing to do just that if it was the sacrifice needed for people like my father to continue to do what they do.

I don't know if I ever told my father how much of an impact he had on my choice to join the Army. It's not something I even like to talk about, because when I look back, it eats me alive thinking of the type of life and opportunities that I threw away before I left. I see all kinds of men and women who joined the military for a job or for college tuition, and I had all of that handed to me and wasted it. My father preached to me that no matter what happens, I always have the opportunity to pick myself up, dust myself off, and try again; that I can change the course of my life. At that moment in my life I saw two options; continue down the path of self-destruction, or put my heart and soul into something...every ounce I had left in me to show not only my family, but the world, who Tim Natale is.

I will never forget the day I was approached by the recruiter on Kent State's campus. My relationship with my girlfriend Kelsey Rose was in the dumps, and I had just failed a test that I put no effort into passing. The only way I was able to keep my head up throughout the day was because every night I was still coaching with my dad.

The recruiter came up to me and asked "Have you ever thought about the joining the Army?" Little did this guy know, I was G.I. Joe for Halloween until I was probably 20 (convenient enough the year I enlisted). But he was asking me as a man not a boy. This guy was clearly new because he had no idea how to pitch to a group of entitled college kids. Turns out I didn't require much "pitching." I met with the recruiter the next day in his office across the street from campus, soon to find out I was his first "contract" and that was his first day. Two hours later I was calling my dad to tell him "I'm joining the Army Reserves!"

Self-entitled son who has nothing to show for himself in school calls his incredibly successful father to inform him that all of his beyond generous tuition money will be wasted not only because I was failing my classes, but because I was joining the Army. He was furious. I had no clue what I wanted to do in the Army Reserves. I bounced around from truck driver to like 40 other jobs. I didn't care because I knew this was my chance; my chance to show my father what I was made of and more importantly that even though I threw most of my previous opportunities away, this was going to be different. I was going to make him proud. I know for certain I have never told my father this; in fact, he will be hearing it for the first time when he reads this chapter: I wanted my father to look at me the same way I looked at him. I was so proud of my father. I adored my father. I idolized my father, my father is my hero and I prayed one day that would be mutual...and this was my chance.

Eventually I made the decision that if I was going to join the military, I was going active duty. I was going to give the Army 4 years of my life and pour my heart and soul into every single day of it. I was going to show my father that I hadn't wasted everything he taught me and that there was still hope. Despite his extreme hesitancy and encouragement to rethink my choice, I enlisted in November of 2012, the day that they counted the Presidential votes and confirmed the re-election of President Obama. My father didn't want to see me leave, but he stood by his word that he would support me in whatever I decided to do in life. The week before I left my father had a 30ft flag pole installed in our front yard and has flown the American Flag and United States Army Flag since the day I left. He told me: "That flag will fly high until the day you return home safely."

There aren't enough pages to explain to my father how grateful I am for the life, opportunities, and support he has given me. There definitely are not enough words in the world to tell you everything my father has taught me.

My father is a man of his word, and he has the heart of a lion. Without him I can assure you I wouldn't be the man I am today. I will spend the rest of my life trying to be even half the man my father is, and together he and I will change the world. He showed me what it means to support someone whether you like every choice they make or not. He showed me you don't quit on people until the day God calls us home. He showed me that it's never too late to turn your life around, and that our true purpose in life is to make a difference in the lives of others. Dad you are my hero, and someday I hope you see in me what I see in you. "Amen Amen, I say to you!"

No! Don't Take the Candy Again

One of my biggest pet peeves as a kid is something I'm sure most of you can relate to; it is near impossible to get my mother off of the phone. Personally, I like my phone calls very short and to the point, but that is the exact opposite when it comes to my mother. Something as simple as taking the chicken out of the freezer to thaw is explained to me like she is given me verbal instructions through some complex military communication system on how to land a spaceship on Mars with a remote control. It drove me insane growing up because as a twelve-year-old kid, I believed I knew everything there was to know already. I was thrown a lot to handle early in life, and as I felt I was beginning to get a grasp on it, I began to feel like I should be treated as a man, not as a boy. What I didn't realize is why Moms do that. As much as I wanted to be treated as an adult, there is only so much of an adult you will ever be when it comes to how your mother sees you. This became clear to me the day I graduated basic training. My family came to find me after the ceremony and the first words out of my mother's mouth were "Come here my baby boy..."

Let me take you back a couple of years first. It's critical to this next story that you understand my parents called me "Father Tim" for probably the first eight years of my life. Supposedly I was so good they thought I was going to become a priest. Needless to say, I called an audible on that, and they dropped that idea before I got to the sixth grade. I remember the first day I said a cuss word. Obviously, my brother Nick was involved, but we were outside my house in Twinsburg, and he dropped his Batman action figure and said the casual "Oh shit." I say casual because I believe Nick's first words were cuss words. I started to run inside and tell my mom Nick swore (I was a huge snitch) and he stopped me. His manipulation abilities have always been impressive. He convinced me that "shit" actually wasn't a bad word at all, in fact he provided me with this elaborate story about old English translations getting misunderstood and that is how "shit" got its bad reputation. He got me to say it, and the second I did he ran into the house and told mom. He knew if he ran inside and told on me first, then my statement that Nick swore would hold little credibility. Once again Nick may be a trouble maker, but he is a smart trouble maker.

I was devastated because I was supposed to be the good kid. I mean I was going to be a priest, I couldn't have this incident on my record. I will never forget my mom's reaction. She sent Nick upstairs and pulled me over to the side in the kitchen. She told me "People make mistakes, good people learn from their mistakes and try to help others not make the same ones." I will never forget that day and what she told me that, there had been countless times in my life where I felt I let my mother down and she has always helped me lift myself back up.

I told you my father has always been supportive of me beyond words, and my mother is too, but they have different tactics. Let me just sum it up by saying there is a reason why I brought my mom my report cards vs. dad. There are many instances, however, where I thought my mom lost hope in me. One thing I stood true to is what she told me when Nick and I had troubles early on. She said "Treat people like you would want to be treated, you never know what they have going on. Be kind to people and help them. Stay humble and show compassion, not pity."

I am not a shy person. That grew with age, but I had no issues talking to new people and making friends. This led me to one of the instances where I thought mom would give up on me. Safety Town. For those of you not familiar, safety town is a summer camp essentially where the local Recreation Center teaches young kids how to cross the street, and most importantly how to not talk to strangers. The reason I am so familiar with said program is that I attended twice. Most kids learn the sufficient amount of safety tips the first time, but I am not most kids. The lesson of the day was not to take candy from strangers. They brought this young lady up and introduced her as Megan. She was a counselor at safety town whom I had seen all week. They said she would be playing the role of a stranger and to treat her as a such. Easy enough right? Well, she approached me in the park and said "Hey I'm Megan, would you like some candy?" to which I responded, "Well Megan, that depends on what you got..."

The clever girl had "Glow in the Dark Nerds". Obviously, I took them and being the kind and helpful person my mother taught me to be...I helped her distribution and gave some of the candy to every other kid in the park. Needless to say, I did not pass safety town, and when they counselor asked me why I took the candy and passed it out I said

"Well she's not a stranger, she's Megan and you don't just pass up on "Glow in the Dark Nerds. My mom told me you have to help people, so I helped her." I failed safety town not once but twice. For the exact same reason, but the second time my mom was waiting in the trees watching me. I know she was in the trees because as I took the candy again, I heard her yell "No! Don't take the candy again!" She cried so hard that night, came balling home to my dad. Looking back, I don't think helping a stranger distribute candy to other kids in the park is what she meant by being kind and helpful. Reflecting back on her teaching me such simple lessons is a huge reason why I found some of the success I did in the Army. Those simple characteristics are universal, among cultures, countries, professions...treating people the way my mother taught me to is something I will take with me anywhere I go.

My mom always found a way to keep me humble. Whether it was on the phone like I said earlier, or more complicated times as I grew she reminded me that you couldn't go it alone, like my father says "everyone needs a cheerleader in life." She taught me to lean on my brothers especially. Even with my friends, she found a way to make us closer. She always reminded me that she is still my mom, and I will always need her motherly ways. As tough as I thought I was growing up, she kept me level headed. Arrogance can destroy a person. I swear like a sailor but to my defense, my Drill Sergeant told me "they are not curse words...they are sentence enhancers." Even though the priest thing didn't work out so well, she kept my head on my shoulders and guided me. I will never forget when I came home on leave for the first time. I was given an extra ten days of leave if I helped the local recruiters during the day. I came in the house and before I could get my boots off she called me over "Hey Timmy, come here I have to tell you a secret." I should have known what was coming; she had been doing this since I was a kid. She would put her arm around my shoulder and start walking with me. When I leaned in for the secret, she would throw me to the ground with some Bruce Lee style hip toss. To this very day, I have no idea where she learned that, but without fail, it works on me and all my friends every time. She looked down at me and said: "you may be a tough soldier, but I'm still your mom, and I can kick your ass." As tough and smart as you may think you are, stay humble. Arrogance brings complacency, and there is always someone in this world who is smarter and tougher than you are.

My mother and I have had our fair share of good times as I grew up, but we had our rocky moments as well. She and I struggled seeing eye to eye with a lot of things. Most mothers probably do with teenage boys, but the majority stemmed from the struggles I had with Nick. Some of the best talks my mother and I have had were about my brothers. She has seven brothers of her own. Unfortunately, some of her brothers have dealt with some substance abuse issues, and she has spent a significant amount of time trying to support them as much as possible. She has helped me with so much. I will take care of my brothers until the day God calls me home, but she taught me there will be times when I would have to let help themselves. As I sit and watch the men both of my brothers are becoming, it's hard to sit back and let them fend for themselves. Especially Dominic. When I left for the Army he was so small and feeble, now three and a half years later he is about to graduate college and there's no doubt he will lead an extremely successful life.

Most of all she has helped me with my brother Nick. As much as he struggles, she helped me realize he has to want to help himself. It's hard to watch someone you care about fall on their face time and time again, but you can only hold them up for so long. My mother is one of my biggest fans, and I am hers. She keeps me level and on the right path. I think of her like a boxing coach, and me the boxer. She follows me wherever I want to go, regardless of how much it may sting for her to watch. I can't imagine it's easy for any mother to watch their son leave for the Army, or be overseas away from him for two years but she did it.

Like the coach and the boxer, she lets me fight my fights, and when I am tired and weak, I come to my corner where she is waiting patiently. She gives me what I need to get back into the ring, reminds me I'm doing ok and to get back out there and try again. That's the reason why moms coddle their sons. As tough as I think I am, as tough as a boxer may be, I come back to my corner when I am in need and overtime she is sitting there patiently willing to lift me back up and guide my back into the ring because she believes in me and my strength. It doesn't mean your weak when you can't stand, even the strongest people fall, but just think of how many football teams, boxers, or athletes in general have gone on to win the big game or fight after a pep talk from their coach. Once again you can't go through life on your own, everyone needs a coach, friend, mentor, hero to help lift them up when they fall, and help them celebrate when they succeed.

The Champ is Down but He's Not Out

It would be easier to capture sunlight in a glass jar than to articulate all I have learned from my Grandfather (Papi). I have realized, though, like the sun, you don't capture it, it nourishes you every day.

Papi is the core of our family, even though roughly the last decade of his life he spent in and out of hospitals, treatment centers, and a wheel chair. He passed away on September 20th, 2015, and I can honestly say it may have been one of the only funerals where I have seen people smile because they truly believed he was in a better place. You are never ready to lose someone you love, but he spent every minute of every day trying to change the lives of those around him. He was the happiest man I ever knew, even while fighting some of the toughest battles I have ever seen fought. People were proud to have met him even once, and God blessed me with the opportunity to call him my grandfather, he is to this very day my hero.

I remember at his wake, people coming up to me and telling me they had known my grandfather longer than I have been alive; and that through all the years that had passed – he was still the same man they knew decades ago. I was impacted the most when a young man had come up to me crying and told me he was the man who cleaned the floors in my grandfather's assisted living center. He went on to tell me how my Papi was the only person that he

27

could 100% guarantee would be smiling every day, and Papi greeted him by name when he walked in every morning. It was amazing, someone who barely knew my grandfather, someone my grandfather could have easily overlooked, had come to the wake just to tell us all how much Papi had impacted his life with something as simple as knowing his name and saying hello. Mother Teresa said, "not all of us can do great things, but we can do small things with great love." My grandfather did incredible things in his life, everything he did was done with the purest love, but he chose to make the time to do the smallest things that greet that man with a hello, because he knew it would make that man smile, even for a moment. My father always tells our football team "God puts people in your life sometimes for a moment, sometimes for a season, sometimes for a lifetime."

Papi and I had always been close, and for the early years of my life, I attribute that to our mutual interest in baseball. Papi played baseball for the Navy, then went on to play a few years on the farm team for the New York Yankees so it's safe to say he may have had a little more talent than me. Papi was the definition of a role model. He used to always tell me "You need to find a woman who loves you like Nani loves me." Let's say I have done my fair share of "research" into finding the right woman.

One day in late spring after my freshman year of college I strolled into my mother's store in Chagrin Falls called Dazzle. She had this beautiful young girl working for her, who she felt compelled to introduce me to; her name, Kelsey Rose. Me being the kind hearted stellar gentleman I am felt compelled to flirt with her. Long story short we started dating. Something was different, and I knew I had to tell me, grandpa. He would be so proud when I told him "This woman is different, Papi."

Mind you Papi never cared what you called to talk about, he just loved hearing his grandkids call on the phone. I called him and began to tell him how great Kelsey Rose was, but getting Papi to concentrate was a feat in itself. Nani was yelling in the background for him to take his medicine, and eventually, he proceeds to tell me, "Well I better get going before your grandmother kills me so why don't you just call me tomorrow and we will talk."

The sneaky guy used the same line of me every day for the next week. Before you know it months had gone by and Papi and I had talked on the phone every single day.

Two years passed and my grandfather, and I still spoke on the phone every single day. It was only for a minute or two each day, but it was amazing. I could be having the worst day, and he would pick up the phone happy as ever. Every time he would answer and call me something different. "Timmmmmmy" or "T-bone", sometimes I even got "Timmy Tim Tim! Then when he ran out of names, he would just pick random words to greet me with when he answered the phone like "okkkkkkk" and "alrighty." It was all I needed to get through some tough days.

The best days were when Nani would answer all frustrated and tell me "Papi tried to answer the TV remote again when the phone rang, so I had to answer for him."

My grandpa and I became so close, and it all started from that simple conversation about Kelsey Rose. When I told him I was joining the Army, he was so proud. I had terrible grades, and my dad and I had struggled with our relationship because of it, but Papi never quit on me. He made it seem so simple he would just tell me "Well keep trying."

When I joined the military, he knew it would be different. He knew why I was going. In fact, I think my Papi is the only person I told the whole reason I joined the military. He was the strongest man I have ever met. Spent the better half of two decades in and out of hospitals, I can't even count a number of times they didn't think he would make it. I think he used up all of our family miracles, though. The doctors told him years before I enlisted he would never stand on his own again.

The last few months before I went to basic training I took Papi to all of his appointments. I got to drive the handicap van; Nani would ride shotgun, and he would be in his wheelchair in the back making race car noises as I drove down the highway. You just couldn't keep this man from enjoying every single moment he spent on this earth. I would ask him if he was in pain and he would respond "Oh it could always be worse." Every single night for those 4 or five months before I left my father, and I went over to their house and helped Papi get into bed, but one night was special.

My dad called me down into his office and told me not to freak out, but Papi had fallen. He was ok, but he didn't want me to tell my brothers because he didn't want everyone to start getting all worried. Dad and I loaded up and drove over to see Nani pacing in the house, and Papi naked laying on the floor next to his bed. He sees us and with a smile that could light up the world says "The champ is down, but he's not out!" I have never laughed so hard in my life. We were all so nervous, afraid he was seriously hurt. Nani looked like she may black out herself, and all he has to say is "the champ is down, but he's not out!"

If that story doesn't describe everything you need to know about Papi, then I'm not sure what will. He was beaten up, confined to a wheel chair, in more pain than I could ever imagine, and all he can think about is how to make us smile and to make sure we knew that he still hadn't quit. Papi hadn't stood by himself in probably three years. The day I left for basic my grandfather stood to hug me goodbye. No walker, no help, he stood on his own and put his St. Anthony medal around my neck. He told me he was proud of me, and that no matter what happened he loved me and that if he wasn't allowed to quit, neither was I.

On May 9th, 2013 I graduated basic training. He was there. My grandfather made a 10-hour drive despite every doctor telling him not to. He never was a good listener. My grandpa coming to that graduation meant the world to me; he refused to miss it. Papi got a chance to meet Chris Doyle and some of the greatest men and women on this planet. He also got a chance to put a face to Drill Sergeant Brito. When Papi said he was going to do something, he did it... and there he was waiting for me to graduate.

His spirit was invincible, and his personality, unrivaled. He changed the world every single day he was alive. I spoke to my grandpa every single day until the day he died. He taught me so much; he showed me life is as great as you make it. He showed me you couldn't beat someone who will not quit. He had a smile on his face every moment of every day. Every single award I got, I thought about Papi.

How proud he would be. Papi passed away six weeks after my two-year tour in Germany. I was so afraid he would pass when I was overseas and not get a chance to come home, but he held on for me.

Two years overseas we spoke nearly every day. Very few times I would be in a country where I wouldn't be able to call him, and that was tough, but the moment I was back in Germany he was the first person I called. Two years and he still couldn't figure out the time difference was six hours. Every single day he would pick some random amount of time he thought was the difference and he was clever. He would ask me when I thought I would be home again to see him but he would only ask if Nani wasn't around to holler at him for the asking.

"So, um, when do you think, you may, um, be coming around these parts, of the um, world.... anytime soon ya think?" I never got annoyed with him asking me; I loved it. It meant he missed me as much as I missed him and I would tell him every single time "I'll be home before you know it."

I had told my friends that the unfortunately anticipated day Papi passed away would cripple me. I couldn't imagine my life without my grandfather, especially the joy he brought me every day when we spoke. Towards the end he began to truly find himself confused, he was weak, but he hung on until I had completed my tour. The few days before Papi had passed my father and I spoke daily, I knew the days were limited, but you still can never prepare yourself enough.

When the phone rang Sunday morning, I knew. Papi had passed away. I didn't cry; I knew my father and I would rely on each other to stay strong, but something was different. I was sad because he was gone, but I didn't cry. Papi passed away during a chicken wing commercial. You laugh, but he chose when it was time for him to go. As insane as it sounds, my grandfather passed away when a commercial came on of his absolute favorite food. Very few people leave this earth and still find a way to make those around them smile, and I would imagine even fewer decide to leave when a food commercial comes on.

This just adds to the way my grandfather lived. Literally, until the moment he left this earth, he made everyone smile. No doubt in my mind he changed this world. I joke that Papi must have called in all of his favors his first few hours in heaven because not only did the Cleveland Browns win, but my dad's football team won for this first time that year as well. My father went to coach that game that day because he knew his dad would have wanted that. I knew what my Papi would want from me too. I went to Buffalo Wild Wings and ate more chicken wings than any human should consume on their own.

I was at peace when my grandfather passed. It wasn't the hell that I thought it would be without him. I call my Nani every day now because she has that glow that he had, she loves beyond limits; she is the strongest women I know. I promised my grandfather I would take care of her and I will. My grandfather left his legacy here on earth for his family to fulfill. Every day when I speak to my grandmother, it reminds me of him, and how he treated her, it reminds me exactly how I will treat to a woman I spend the rest of my life with. She reminds me every day what he taught me all those years.

I will take care of Nani; I promise Papi. I will never forget what he said to me the day my friend was killed just weeks before Papi himself passed. It was like he knew he wouldn't be here much longer himself. He told me "all this means is that he has a better spot to watch you change the world, pick up the torch and lead the way." The world will never be the same without you Papi, you have left big shoes to fill, but I will lead the way.

The Queen

There is not a person in my family who has the guts to question who runs the whole family, its grandma...Nani. She is by far the most incredible women I have ever met, and I am not just saying that because she scares me. There is a story that I think describes Nani perfectly so let me set the scene for you.

When my father was in Law school, my mother and he had been dating a few years and my mom came back with my dad for the summer to work at Nani and Papi's bar. They owned this bar called "The Beer and Belly Deli." Mom was waitressing and living with my dad's Aunts just down the road from his house. He was over his aunt's house watching a movie with my mom, and when they movie was over he came wondering home. Mind you he's in probably his first or second year of Law school so let's say he's 23 or 24. He comes wondering in at eight after midnight he says and as he's taking off his shoes he recalls getting knocked to the ground by a blunt object. Nani had thrown a frying pan down the stairs and hit him in the head because he was late. She's yelling and tells my dad "I thought you were dead, you didn't call. Only hoodlums are out at midnight at your age."

My grandmother is an absolute saint. She was by Papi's side every single step of the way. She is a testament to what it means to truly love someone. Nani and Papi set the precedent for our family and how love is supposed to be. As great a woman as she is, she is a fireball. Italian women are beautiful, but also angry...beautifully angry. There is no escaping Nani and her questions either. School, college, girlfriends, military it doesn't matter when grandma asks you a question you better answer, and more importantly answer truthfully. It's like an interrogation chamber when she gets going.

My grandmother and I have grown pretty close. I give her a hard time, but we get along great. To this very day, she still tells me I cuss to much, but remember what my drill sergeant said, they are sentence enhancers not cuss words. The last year or so before Papi passed away she began to answer the phone for him every day when I called. I would always smile because I could hear them bickering in the back ground. "No Anthony, that's the damn TV remote your trying to answer.... here's the phone right here." As I said, her and I still speak daily and it's the highlight of my day. We talk about things like her golf game (sensitive subject) and her joining the choir (also sensitive subject). The best part is because of how long Nani was by Papi's side, I believe she actually thinks she is a board certified medical doctor. She will give you a diagnosis and elaborate medical treatment plan for every little cut you have on your knee. The best part of it is, she is adamant that she is always right and "those damn doctors just don't know what they are talking about".

As much as I joke with Nani, she is someone who I am beyond lucky to have in my life. The last decade or so as I grew older I sat and watched how she treated Papi. They bickered, but the love she had for him is something like I have never seen before. When Papi told me to find woman like Nani to spend the rest of my life with, she's leaving some serious shoes to fill. Watching the way she treated him was moving. Saying goodbye to my grandfather was one of the toughest parts when leave was over, but knowing she was with him made it just a bit easier.

I have made some mistakes in my life. I had a period in my life when I thought I needed a new girlfriend every few weeks to be cool. When I started to get attention from women in high school, I thought that was the cool thing to do. I will never forget when Nani called me out in front of everyone. I had been dating a young lady in high school and we broke up. No big deal, things happen but when one of my cousins asked me about it at the dinner table I made some snappy response like 'Oh who cares, on to the next'. Nani looked at me and said "When are you going to get your life together?" I felt like it was a little brutal, but looking back it was perfect. She never tip toed around her thoughts, and she wasn't just talking about my comment about the girlfriend. If Nani did one thing, she held me accountable. School, women, life . . . she expected more out of me and had no problem telling me.

The day of Papi's funeral I was slow to start the day. My father had taken me to get these two incredible suits. I had injured my back, which we will get to later, and I could barely put on my own pants. Nani found a way to smile the entire night before at the wake. Despite his medical conditions and the care required, she knew they had such an incredible relationship. The way he looked at her was like out of a movie. She told all of us how much Papi would want us to enjoy our time together, and that she didn't want to see anyone upset. I took the top off my Wrangler because Papi had blessed us with such a beautiful day I couldn't help but enjoy that weather. He always told Nani when he passed he did not want her to wear black. He said she was too beautiful for such a dark color. As slow of a start as I was having, when I saw Nani that morning it all turned around. She had been married to him for over 50 years, if she was smiling so could I. She listened to Papi and wore this beautiful red dress. Even after he passed, she did everything she possible could to make him the happiest man in the world.

Love like that is precious. My father always said love without limits. Nani set the precedent. She is the strongest women I know. She held me accountable and believed in me when I didn't even believe in myself. There is no doubt in my mind that the love that she had for Papi is what gave him strength in those tougher days. Every step of the way she was right there by his side, and as fiery as she can be...I wouldn't have it any other way.

Brothers Fight

My older brother Nicholas is responsible for some of the worst memories I have, but he is also the core of why I strive to be the best man I can be. My brother Nick has had his fair share of rough battles so far, but he is a resilient man. He doesn't always make the best choices, and he and I haven't always been as close as we are today, but I would not trade him for the world. My brother Nick has saved me more times than I can count, and I attribute a lot of my success to him and our experiences. I don't make a lot of money, and I don't mean success in a material sense, I mean success in being able to move past obstacles which seem impossible to overcome. Six or seven years ago, I would have told you I didn't care if I ever spoke to Nick again, but something changed. Nick taught me the true importance of brotherhood, and I will take that to my grave. My brothers are my world, and it took me a long time to realize just how important they were.

Nick has battled disorders ranging from simple learning disorders to personality and mood disorders. As you can imagine, these types of struggles affect more than just Nick, and for a while our family infrastructure spiraled downhill rapidly. I used to tell my friends my family was like a magazine cover, because we looked great on the cover

39

but you had no idea what was inside until you took the time to open it. We had a big house, money, cars, nice clothes, but there were years I dreaded coming "home." Nick and I had years where we spoke only when absolutely mandated, because even though Nick had his struggles, all I saw was how it affected me. Nick would annoy my friends, or he and I would fight, to what seemed to be, to death. For years, I blamed the tension in our house on Nick. Nick did this; Nick did that; Nick started it; and 99% of the time he did. I had alienated my brother because he wasn't like me, and that's all that I cared about. I didn't realize Nick took the blame the other 1% of the time. He never said Tim hit me first, or Tim broke the lamp. He made every excuse in the world about why he made all the mistakes he made, in every aspect of his life except me: he never blamed me.

Nick had a way of making my life more complicated than it needed to be. I made friends with an upperclassman in football camp going into my freshman year, and I was going to be the cool kid who hung out with older guys. Man, was I wrong because my first day of high school someone threw an apple at Nick from behind. Something in Nick's wiring told him "Hey Nick, just turn around and punch the first person you see right in the face." You guessed it, Nick punched one of my only friends right in the face, and from that day forward I was known as Nick Natale's brother.

Nick and I fighting was not normal sibling rivalry. If it was, then the cops would not have known our names each time they were called. When we fought, it was brutal, and for years all we saw was hatred towards each other. We neglected the fact that our little brother Dominic was sitting in the corner watching our family unfold.

I will never forget the 4th of July the year before I went to college, when Nick and I had a fight for the ages. I saw red, and it was one of the worst fights I have been in in my entire life. My mother called the police, and we spent what seemed like an eternity on the driveway until my father came home to see the police cars in the driveway. My heart sank, because, up until this point, all I had really worried about was myself. When Nick made me mad, we fought; when Nick annoyed me, we fought. I was just filled with anger. My family was falling apart, and I knew I had a huge role in our demise. Our bonus room was over the garage with a window that looked into the driveway. That night I had caught a glimpse of the window and saw my little brother Dominic with tears rolling down his face. My mother was a mess, and my dad had pure disappointment in his eyes, embarrassed because two of his sons had the police involved. I did what I do best, blamed it all on Nick, got in my car, and left to go to my Uncle Carl's house for the family 4th of July party. I left the mess I made behind, and Nick was left there to take the fall once again.

I spent the next month living at my uncle's house, because I just needed to get away. By the time I came home in August, I had about a week until I left for my first year of college, and I couldn't have been more afraid. I hated being home, but I had never been on my own before, so as much as I wanted to get away, I had no idea how to handle myself. I remember sitting in my room and wondering how my little brother Dom was going to handle me going away. We had built this unity and up until the day I left, we had gone through some of the toughest moments together. What I feared even more was if, when I was gone, I would get the call that Nick's depression had finally beat him, and Nick had succeeded in his quest to take his own life. This haunted me, because as much as I "hated" Nick, I couldn't shake the fact that I could never imagine my life without him. Nick and I fought like hell, but that was just it, it was Nick and I fighting, no one else. Nick and I could fight to the death, but there still was this instinct that if the time came where someone else picked a fight with one of us, it didn't require words to know we were on the same team, even if it was just for that moment.

I sat there on the floor of my room and remembered back years ago, when Nick and I both attended St. Rita Elementary school. I must have been in 2nd grade or so, but Nick and I were at recess at the same time. This was the same year Fox 8 News interviewed the two of us on sibling rivalry. We were not friends, and we sure as hell didn't get along, but brothers are still brothers.

Four-square was the game of choice that year, and there was an understood rule that anyone could play as long as they waited in line until someone got out. I was always the smallest kid, and each day I waited in line until it was my turn, but each day it was like the bell knew I was next and would ring right when it was my turn. Finally, the day came and it was my turn and I had this over whelming joy rush over me. It didn't matter if I got out immediately, all I wanted to do was play. As I took the step in, this big chubby kid in Nick's grade pushed me out of the way and claimed he had been waiting in line but had just ran inside to use the bathroom. I knew this wasn't the truth, but it was my word against a fourth grader's. I didn't have the fire in me nor the anger I did when I grew older. I walked to the corner of the building and just sat there and began to cry. As wimpy as it sounds, it was the truth.

Out of nowhere came the brother I "hated" who may be weighed one pound more than I did. Nick was every bit of fifty pounds lighter than the chubby old bully, but Nick was angry. He must have seen the whole thing, because Nick took that kid to the ground with a tackle that made the ground shake. Nick was normally an angry kid because he thought he was different, but this was a different type of angry. This was an angry I had not seen before. This was anger from watching his little brother get thrown down, and watching the tears come pouring down my face.

Nick didn't have friends at St. Rita; he was on every teacher's radar, and he and I both knew he was going to get scolded when he got home, but none of that mattered to him. Nick may not even remember this happening, but after the whooping he gave that kid, he just came and sat down next to me. I could take you this very day to the exact square on the sidewalk where we sat. He didn't say a word to me; he just sat there to let me know I wasn't alone, and waited there until the teachers came to get him. To this day, Nick struggles taking responsibility for his actions; we all do. That day, Nick didn't fuss, he didn't make excuses. When the teachers came to get him, he stood up like a man, and took the punishment because he knew what he did; he did for me.

We got home that night, and of course the teachers had called the house. Nick didn't explain why he did what he did, he just took it. He was young, but instinct is something you're born with. Nick taught me that, he taught me that whether you like them or not, brothers are brothers. I lost track of that for a long time, but I remembered that story vividly when I was sitting on my floor that day. That summer was definitely a low point for Nick and me, and I knew it was time to take the leap toward fixing us, not just for Nick and me, but for my family too.

I wrote Nick a letter that must have been 10 pages and slid it under his door. I couldn't get myself to go sit down with him and talk face to face. My heart felt like it was beating a million miles an hour, but it was time. I went back and sat in my room and was just looking out the window when I heard "Nick steps". Nick didn't walk in the house like most people. Even on the stairs, you knew when it was Nick coming. If a person's footsteps could be angry, Nick's were. He came and stood at the door of my room and the letter in his hand and just stared at me. For once, Nick didn't come barging into my room, he waited at the door for me to invite him to come in. To you, this may not mean a lot, but to me...I saw effort. He was acknowledging the part of my letter where I said we needed boundaries. Nick was listening to me, as simple as it was, Nick was willing to change and so was I.

Nick and I sat in my room for hours and just talked, but Nick asked me to make him a promise I will never forget. Nick asked me to promise him that I will never quit on him. He told me "I will not get this right the first time, or the second..." but all he wanted was to know I would be there. Nick told me "We're brothers, we don't have to like each other, but we need each other" and he couldn't be more right.

Like I said before. my biggest fear was getting a call that Nick had succeeded in taking his own life, and as much as I hated being around Nick at times, my life would be in shambles without him. Nick taught me what it meant to rely on someone, and what an honor it was to truly have someone rely on you with their heart and soul. Nick may be hearing this for the first time when he reads this book, but Nick taught me more than anything I've learned from school or books. Nick showed me what teamwork is, and true brotherhood. Brothers fight, but brothers help each other back up when it's all over.

Nick and I have had a very tough run. I found myself multiple times in my life stuck in a hole, and regardless of the strength I thought I had, I couldn't for the life of me find my way out. Regardless of how dark and hopeless I may have felt, Nick showed me something that may have saved my life. If it wasn't for Nick, I may have never found my way out. He and I had to tackle those obstacles together. Nick's whole life, he has had some serious battles to fight, and he has taken his fair share of his beatings from them, but Nick gets back up and so will I, every single time until the day God calls me home. It's easier to stand when you have someone to stand for. Nick, you told me in a letter you wrote me that you were proud of me, and that you aren't sure you'd be alive if it wasn't for me. Well let me tell you, my friend, brothers share a heartbeat. You and I are in it for the long run. Where we've been has gotten us to where we are, but what really matters is where we are going to go.

DOMSQUAD

I've never been a big fan of saying I look up to someone be-cause people tend to assume you are referring to someone older than you. Fair to say the reason behind my aversion stems from the person I "look up to the most" being my lit-tle brother. Dominic (Boosh) has always found himself tak-ing the blunt of the issues our family shared, and for the longest time, he took an emotional beating from witnessing Nick and my battlefield. It took Boosh a while to find out what type of man he wanted to be, but I absolutely idolize his sense of identity. He is just starting to figure out the number of people who follow his every footstep, and I am the first one behind him I can guarantee that. His nick-name "Boosh" originated from these stupid YouTube videos Dom, my cousin Matt and I used to watch about some stereotypical "gym bro". We used to laugh like there was no tomorrow, but no one came close to Dom's ability to quote these videos with extreme precision.

It seems like just a bunch of friends watching dumb videos with stupid quotes, but it wasn't. The three of us were inseparable and still are. We woke up every day and all went to work at Nied's Garden Center which was owned by my uncle Greg (Matt, Mike, and Rachael's dad). The three of us went to work every day for 8-10 hours, came home and went straight to the gym, and then spent the re-mainder of the night terrorizing my aunt "Lulu" and my other cousins watching these videos. Jokingly we started calling ourselves the "Domsquad" because the group would be absolutely nothing without Dom. He was our identity.

Dom and I are inseparable and have been for as long as I can remember. My biggest fear growing up was letting him down, or letting him make some of the mistakes I did. When I was a senior in high school, Dominic was a freshman and I was responsible for driving him to school. I was in a rough spot in my life emotionally. I didn't really have much respect for myself. Dealing with Nick had taken its toll on me, and I was just going through the motions. Then came the "welcome back dance" which was normally a few weeks before school started up again and I remember the drive like it was yesterday. It was just Dom and I, having a blast and listening to music with the obnoxious speaker system I had in my Toyota Highlander. Dom asked me a question which honestly made my entire year. He asked me if we could get lockers next to each other. Dom and I were great friends and really close but like I mentioned, my biggest fear growing up was letting Dom down. His locker was right next to mine; I had no choice but to make the change in order to be the brother that Dom deserved.

So many times in my life I have wondered what my purpose could be. Most young men and women do this same thing as they grow, but I found myself wondering at a deeper level and questioning if I even had a purpose. That day when Dom asked me to get lockers next to each other might honestly have been the best day of my life. It sounds trivial, but I couldn't explain the feeling I would get those days when Nick and I used to fight and I would leave the house knowing Dom was left there with my mess. For the longest time, I honestly thought there could be no way Dominic would forgive me. When Dom came to high school I promised myself it would be different: I would be different because he relied on me to lead the way. If there was one thing I knew I would never sell myself short on again, it was being an older brother.

Dom is a huge reason why I found success early in the military. He is a huge reason why I joined the military. I needed to make him proud. I enlisted during his senior year. I wouldn't be at college with him next year, and my only true success thus far in my life was protecting him. That was all I knew, and I wanted nothing more than to continue to do that, whatever the cost may be. He is the reason why I love to lead from the front, because he showed me what my purpose was. He trusted me to clear the way for him. He trusted me to look out for him, but what he didn't realize is what he was actually doing for me. I wasn't the nicest person to people in school. I didn't have good grades, and can't remember one week when I didn't have at least one detention. I came to school depressed, and my friends were great about it, but having my little brother right next to me was all I needed to get through the toughest of days. I couldn't let him see me fall: my strength came from him. I refused to let him make the same mistakes I was. For some reason this is what it took for me to realize the responsibilities that came with being an older brother.

I wasn't the smartest kid and I wasn't the best behaved. At the time, I didn't have much respect for myself. All the pride I had in myself was the relationship I had with Dominic and doing everything I could to be the best role model I could be. I knew I had to change. I would do anything to see him succeed and refused to let him fall into the darkness where I seemed to live. I was angry, and I felt like I was just taking beating after beating emotionally. He had so much in front on him. Dom had everything it took to be the best at whatever he wanted to do and it was my responsibility to get him there. If it meant laying myself over a puddle so he could walk on my back to get safely to the other side then show me where to lay. There was nothing in the world that I was willing to let stop Dom from his dreams.

I had been in such a dark place, but without him even realizing it, Dom gave me purpose. Dom has made every bad mistake I made up to this point worth it because I had an opportunity to help him from making the same ones. For a while it was like a land mine field, telling him where to step, where to avoid, and I'm sure he didn't love that. He helped me realize that life honestly is the ultimate team sport; you can't do it alone. Dom made me feel invincible, but a different type of invincible. He showed me that as dark as my life seemed, as weak as I felt for the longest time, being invincible didn't mean you couldn't be beaten down. It just meant that you couldn't be kept down. He gave me a reason to stand back up and to clear the way. It's crazy the strength you find in yourself when you know someone relies on you to stand in their moment of weakness. I thought my life was tough, but he had taken the worst beating of all from our family issues and he looked to me for strength. My senior year in high school may have been one of the best years of my life. Dom showed me that when obstacles seem absolutely impossible...they may be, but only if you try to overcome them alone. I could tackle anything because I knew Dom was right behind me waiting for me to show him the way; that the coast was clear.

As the years pass and I watch Dominic grow, all I can do is be proud. Before me is a young man who has dealt with unimaginable difficulties in his home life which can cripple even the strongest child's creativity, passion, and desire to explore the world. It would have been so easy for Dominic to just curl up into a ball, and accept a life of mediocracy out of fear of failure and exposure to life's cruelties. Instead, he channeled it in a way I can't even begin to explain to you. His personal identity is something the entire world could learn from. Everyone makes mistakes. They are inevitable in our lives. A true team however, helps each other up when they fall, they hold each other accountable, and rely on each other with their entire heart and soul through the best and worst of times. Obviously as an older brother, it's my job to give my younger brother a hard time, give him the occasional "noogie" and a good old fashioned "Charlie horse" now and then, but as we grow older I just sit back and admire every aspect of the man he is becoming. I owe my little brother my life because, without him, I may have never found my true purpose in the world.

For the longest time, I wondered how I would ever repay Dominic for what he has done for me, up until the moment when I realized I owed no such debt. He didn't treat me the way he treated me because he expected something in return. He did it because it's the type of man he is, it's the type of man my father is, and his father was. I realized that isn't just a characteristic that you pass from generation to generation, it's the type of personality that you change the world with. I sit here some days and look at how dark our world looks, and for a while that's all I did was sit and watch. Essentially, it's the same concept as what I dealt with early in life just on a much bigger scale. The world looks so dark and gloomy and most people just sit back and watch the world we used to know fade away. What would have happened if Dominic just let me fade away? He gave me purpose, he found a way to show that darkness a light that will burn forever. I intend to do the same thing in this world. I will show this darkness a light that cannot be extinguished, I owe that to Dom, because without him I may have just spent my life watching the world go by. Dominic, whether you see it or not, the world spins because of people like you. We are both young and the world has plenty more obstacles to throw our way, but there isn't an obstacle in this world that we can't overcome together.

The Mayor

I know plenty of people who are very close with their cousins, but I've yet to meet any who's relationship compares to that which I have with my cousin Matt Nied. Matt and I are the same age and have grown up absolutely inseparable. I attribute much of my development as a man to Matt. He is as loyal as they come, and I honestly don't think I will ever meet someone I trust anywhere near the way I trust Matt. I have made plenty of bad choices in my life. I have headed down some paths that I am not proud of but Matt Nied has been right by my side every single step of the way. There is not a question in my mind, I would give my life to keep people like Matt Nied safe on this earth because, mark my words, Matt Nied will change the world.

Matt's mother is my Aunt Lynnette (Lulu) who is my dad's sister and my beautiful Fairy Godmother. Matt's dad is my Uncle Greg, Matt's older brother is Michael, and his younger sister is Rachael (Rara). I have yet to find a word to describe their family. They are my saving grace. Matt is about two months younger then I am so, naturally, we became very close at an early age. We caused chaos from the moment we met, and our favorite memory to laugh about is when we were both probably about six years old. We were sitting at a little tykes table, drinking Kool-Aid, and we ran out. Anyone who has consumed Kool-Aid at some point in their life probably is aware that when the moment you run out happens, it's an automatic frenzy. We threw our cups at my mother and yelled "more Kool-Aid" which I'm sure ended terribly for the both of us. This is on home video if you desire to check me on my story, but Matt and I laugh so hard talking about it because of the simplest thing. We were six, but acted the exact same way and said the exact same thing at the exact same time. It seems so minor, but it proves the point that our relationship cannot be duplicated. Matt and I share a heartbeat.

I wish there was a way for me to tell my cousin Matt even a percentage of the impact he made on me growing up. Loyalty doesn't even compare to the way Matt acted towards me. To this very day Matt would give me the shirt off his back without blinking an eye. Something in his brain prevents Matt from considering his own interests over those of the ones he loves. I have tried my entire life so far to find a way to describe to my cousin the way I look up to him, but it seems impossible. He is the walking testament for how to be a son, brother, cousin, or friend. You never really realize how much you can learn from someone your own age.

Matt is a different kind of breed. It's sad that people won't give someone like Matt a chance because they assume he's "too good to be true". I have known Matt for 24 years now and still have yet to find a single thing about Matt that I would classify as a flaw. I mean, the guy wants to be a doctor. Matt could have created a shadow over me that halted any confidence I may have had in myself, but he didn't. Tim McGraw said in one of his songs "When you get where you're going, don't forget turn back around, help the next one in line, always stay humble and kind." Matt is the type of man that would go one step at a time, and turn around to make sure I was right behind him. I owe Matt my life, but he will never collect because Matt does what he does just because he's Matt. Everyone has encountered someone in their life who has some sort of talent or quality that you just can't teach. Ladies and Gentleman I've yet to meet someone on this earth the same breed as Matt Nied.

I worked with Matt multiple summers at his father's garden center and one day I noticed something that literally stopped me in my tracks. We were probably six hours into a hot day of cutting grass, and I was very much looking forward to just sitting in the truck and enjoying the nice lunch my Aunt Lulu was kind enough to make for us. I used to joke with Matt because, for some reason Aunt Lulu would always put mustard on my sandwich even though none of us liked it. I would never complain though because she did make us free lunches every day!

Just like every other morning, I opened my lunch up and would snack on it throughout the day, chewy bars, fruit, yogurt....and I would notice in the morning that once again out of the three of us (Matt, my little brother Dom, and I) I was the only one with mustard. When I finally made my way back to the truck after cutting one of the veterinarian hospitals we were responsible for, I reached in to grab my sandwich. I pulled the wrap off and took an enormous bite, mustard or not I was near starving. No mustard. How could this be, I was 100% positive there was mustard on my sandwich a few hours prior? Out of the corner of my eye Matt is sitting eating his sandwich too, when I noticed yellow mustard dripping out the side. Matt hadn't said anything, he just switched the sandwiches. He didn't want to be recognized for what he did or he would have told me. He just did it. I never even told Matt I noticed. I just remember looking at him and wondering why he does stuff like this, even something so small, without even desiring recognition. Something so minor, I didn't even really get bothered by the mustard, and he wasn't a picky eater, it's just the fact that he knew it may make my day maybe just 1% better than it already was made it all worth it to him. He is the true definition of living to make a difference in the lives of others, whatever cost it may be to him.

My whole life Matt did things like this for everyone, even people he barely knows. As expected, people took advantage of that, even me. You begin to anticipate actions upon repetition. I began to assume Matt would continue to act a certain way. When Matt and I were in high school, I began to get attention from girls. He used to joke with me about it so I used to think I was so cool. Finally, Matt Nied looks up to me about something. Mind you, Matt had straight A's since he was coloring in pre-school and the closest I ever got to a 4.0 GPA was probably in fourth grade - I think I got an A in gym. Matt never got in trouble like I did. His mom used to frisk me for Nerf guns when I came over. If Matt was going to be the smart kid, then I was going to be the tough kid.

The day before I left for boot camp I had a letter typed up for Matt. I must have typed it up 100 different ways but I deleted it. I couldn't find the words to say. I had no idea what the future in the military held for me, or if I would even make it home. I needed Matt to somehow know that there isn't a chance in hell I would be where I was in life without him. He had been my best friend for as long as I can remember. He had pulled me out of some of the darkest moments in my life without even realizing it. Simple acts like switching out those sandwiches that day let me actually take a step back and realize I would give my life to keep him safe. Simple acts like that change the world one person at a time. Just imagine how much the world will change if people like Matt continue to do what they do. I can only imagine the world if everyone was willing to do even the smallest acts like Matt does for nothing other than making someone else's life even just a fraction better.

I remember flying into Poland in the backseat of a Black hawk and we begin our approach, I saw all of these bunkers covered in grass. They had covered the bunkers in grass so enemy planes couldn't tell they were bunkers and hangars when they flew over and bomb them. It wasn't a combat zone, but I was nervous. Suddenly out of nowhere all my nerves went away. I thought about Matt and the summers he, Dominic and I spent cutting grass. All I could think about for that moment was a day when Matt and I were swinging weed whackers around like swords. Thinking back, it wasn't our brightest moment, but I just pictured Matt on these bunkers doing that. I have no explanation why but, just for that moment, that's all it took for the nerves to go away. Just a little smile, and re-living the glory days. Matt had no idea, but he was the reason why that mission went that way it did. Every time I loaded on the aircraft, I saw the bunkers, and Matt gave me the smile I needed. He was my saving grace growing up, and he found a way to keep that going through my brief career in the military. Twelve countries, Matt and our memories followed me to every single one of them.

I wish I had the words to describe to Matt everything he has done for me. He has taught me that it is definitely possible for one person to move mountains, but he has also given me a reason each day to push myself every single moment. He has stood by my side through all of my ups and downs, but most of all, he didn't burry me in his shadow. He gave me the privilege to call it our shadow. Matt, you will change the world buddy and I promise you I will be right by your side when you do.

Michael, Michael, Motorcycle...

My cousin Matt and his older brother are nothing alike personality - wise, but one thing I can tell you they do share is the potential to absolutely change the world. It's wild how sometimes in life we tend to overlook the people who hold us together, we take them for granted. In my family that is my cousin Michael (Mikey). First of all, no matter how intense and stressful our stereotypical Italian family get togethers can be, there is no way to avoid smiling when Mikey comes twirling in the room. I say twirling because Mikey dances everywhere and is actually surprisingly graceful. Twenty-four years into my life, Mikey is still the only person I know who takes the "I'll buy a new shirt when this one falls off my body" phrase literally. Don't get me wrong, he cleans his shirt, and is a surgeon with a tide to go stick, but he wears these shirts that look like they have been target practice for a machine gun.

Mikey is the type of man that flies under the radar. He doesn't like to draw attention to himself. Mikey and I have always gotten along, but as I started to grow a bit older, probably towards the end of high school, I realized just how much I looked up to Mikey. I have come to Mikey for a wide variety of issues in my life. Mikey got one of the best traits from Papi - his unprecedented ability to light up every room he enters. When you have someone with that

58

type of personality as the foundation of a family, it's impossible for family feuds to last. Someone like Mikey has taught me the ability to brush off some of the toughest moments in my life and to realize just how important happiness is and what it truly means to be happy and comfortable with yourself.

When Mikey was little, the only way to truly upset him was to do one of two things. I have to admit I participated in both, but all in good fun. One was to steal his stuffed pink power ranger, and the other was to sing this little song to him... "Michael Michael, motorcycle, turn the key and watch him pee." I genuinely have no idea where it came from, so we will just blame his brother Matt. Recently, even as a kid, Mikey didn't care what people said about him. We lose sight of that in today's world, trying to conform to what we perceive as "social norms." I never really realized it until looking back, but growing up I probably followed every "social norm" there was. It's not necessarily a bad thing, but I genuinely envy Mikey's authenticity. Twenty plus years later he still has Brittany Spears all over his Facebook, he still dances around the living room, and still the guy never sleeps in a bed. I am jealous of people like Mikey who can wake up every single day and do what makes them happy with no concern for anyone else's opinions. We all smile at times, but a smile like Mikey's comes from the soul, and a smile like his will change the world.

From being in the military I can pretty much sleep anywhere, but this guy still has me beat. I remember when I went with Mikey's family to Hilton Head when I was in college. Dominic came too, and every morning I would wake up either hung over, or rubbing my eyes walking into the bathroom and I would trip and fall. When I stood back up I would realize I tripped over Mikey. The guy would bring his pillows and blankets into the bathroom and sleep on the floor. He has been doing this for years. He sleeps in the wildest places in the house: laundry rooms, bathrooms, living rooms, you name it he has slept there. Anytime you ask him why he will tell you he was up late and didn't want to wake anybody up sneaking into the room, or because he snores too loud: I know plenty of you who are reading this snore, but how many of you would sleep on a tile floor just to avoid the possibility of waking someone up? It speaks to the sincerity and genuine heart of my cousin Mikey.

For the summers I spent working at my uncle's garden center, Mikey would normally work in the front office or desk and was the first person a customer would see when they walked in. Let me tell you if I owned a business of any kind, Mikey would be the first person I would want people to see. Michael would dance everywhere, spinning in circles, skipping, twirling...and that is exactly how he would great these people. I am not making fun of him, it is the most incredible thing I have ever seen. People love him because he is the nicest person you will ever meet - so gentle and kind. He smiles from ear-to-ear and every inch of it is pure and sincere. So often in our lives, we find ourselves either running into people, or being the person ourselves, who puts on a mask for work, school, sports, whatever just to "please" everyone else. It scarcely works because as people we learn to read sincerity and look right through the molds our world has created. If you take a moment when you are speaking to someone to actually pay attention, you begin to notice when people deploy these "temporary masks" and you begin to question the sincerity of their actions or words.

Twenty-four years of my life have passed and I have yet to question the genuine nature of my cousin Mikey. His happiness in himself is unprecedented. If he enjoys it, you'll know. He doesn't fall subject to these molds and standards that society wants us to adopt. He is his own man, and an incredible one at that. His ability to enjoy even the smallest things in life is an ability a lot of us begin to lose as the years go on. As young kids, we enjoy everything and as much as kids cry, they laugh even more. Mikey is the type of man who never lost that ability, and he can light up the room with it just like my Grandpa could.

There is never a dull moment when Mikey is around, and he has been such a huge source of happiness for me my entire life. I look forward to every opportunity I get to spend some time with him. The laughs and the good times we have will never fade. Mikey, I know I don't really need to tell you this, but keep doing what you're doing Stay true to yourself and keep the good times flowing. Just like Papi, you have the ability to light up the world with your personality, and I wouldn't trade that for anything.

The Three Stooges

I'm well aware that the three stooges were men, but it just fit so perfectly to describe my three beautiful girl cousins. Rachael is the youngest of the three; she is Matt and Michaels little sister. Brittani is Carl's daughter, CJ and Anthony's sister, and Emily is from my mother's side of the family, she is my Uncle John and Aunt Donna daughter. I have more girl cousins on my mother's side of the family, but unfortunately, I was never as close with them as I was with Emily. Emily lived a few hours away from us growing up but would come up for summers and spent enough time up here that she might as well be a Natale. See I don't have any sisters, so girl cousins were as close as it got. I always have been very protective of them like sisters of my own, "the women in your family should be treated as gold" as Papi used to say. Through some of my younger days, I didn't always realize that applied to all women, not just my family. As protective as I was of my own, I was also hypocritical. When I thought it was the cool thing having a new girlfriend every few weeks, I didn't realize the example I was setting. I also didn't realize just how hypocritical it was to act this way and not understand these women I dated had families of their own telling them to avoid guys like me. The women I dated were cousins, daughters, sisters and grandkids of someone else's family.

When my cousins got to the age where boys started to come around, I had my fair share of stresses, except with Brittani. She was a black belt when she was like seven so she was a little less worrisome. When she brought a boyfriend around, I normally felt inclined to protect them from her.

As protective as I was, there were times where I was over protective. For the longest time, there was nobody that would ever be good enough for my cousins. I'm sure a lot of you can relate to this, sisters, daughters, etc. This feeling that nobody will ever meet the criteria you have set for them when in fact there are no criteria. I just remember this one day when Emily had a crush on some guy, and I did something to upset her. She was arguing with me about how I was too protective, and I just kept telling her 'he doesn't deserve you.' Her response stopped me in my tracks. She said, "well you don't always treat girls the best either, you have a new girlfriend every other week!" We were sitting by the pool in my back yard, and she got up and stormed off. I wanted to call after her but I couldn't, there was nothing to say...she was right.

All these years I had been doing what I thought was best for them while simultaneously being an incredible hypocrite. I sat there ripping apart every aspect of these guys they brought home when in turn I was telling them to avoid nearly everything about myself. It's so easy in life to judge other people, to make comments for others best interests, to tell others what they are doing wrong, but my Uncle Carl told me something that I will never forget. He told me "It takes a big man to admit when he's wrong, and let me tell you there aren't a lot of big men in this world."

As I've mentioned before, there was a point when I had little to no respect for myself, but times like these made me look into that mirror. I had to look at myself and confront the flaws I had been avoiding. I had to confront the flaws I pointed out with these young men my cousins met when intact they were also flaws of my own.

See in middle school I was just cute little Tim Natale. I weighed about 75 lbs. when I graduated eighth grade. By no stretch was I much heavier throughout high school but when I began to get attention from women it got to my head. As harmless as it seemed at the time, I was a jerk and Emily was right. It's was so easy for me to sit up on my self-created pedestal and tell Emily, Rachael, and Brittani what type of man they deserved. It was the classic 'do as I say, not as I do' mindset. I would tell them what was "wrong" with every guy they had the slightest crush on until I realized I was indirectly telling them to avoid guys like me. The concept of this book is to appreciate the characteristics and lessons you learn from people and experiences in your life; while sharing with you some of mine. That day when Emily called me out was quite a wakeup call to just that.

Rachael probably got the worst of my over protectiveness because she was around the most. Emily got her fair share to when she was around in the summers, and we spoke a lot on the phone. When I say, I'm pretty sure the majority of Brittani's boyfriends were afraid of her I mean it. I sat back that day and thought about what Emily said to me. All I wanted was for them to grow up and have a relationship like Nani and Papi, full of happiness and respect. To truly be appreciated for who they were, and be treated like they were the only woman on the earth. They were the princesses of the family, and they deserved to be treated like that, every woman does. How could I be telling them this, when I wasn't treating the women I dated like that. One of the hardest things I have ever had to do in my life was to look in the mirror and admit when I was wrong. It's no epiphany that everyone has flaws and shortcomings, but that's what makes the human race so great is the ability to change.

We have the ability to grow into whatever and whomever we want to be, at any point in our lives. It's never too late to change unless you let it be by accepting what your current situation as your fate. I knew the day would come when I found the girl I wanted to spend the rest of my life with and my three cousins helped me realize that as I grew older, that day was drawing near. When it did, was I going to keep acting like an arrogant little jerk that I was telling them to avoid...or would I admit my flaws and turn into the man I tried to help them find. Mahatma Gandhi said, "be the change you want to see in the world." I couldn't think of any better quote to fit this book, and especially this chapter. It was so easy for me to ride by on my high horse and act like my wisdom came from some noble prophet, but it wasn't until I realize the only way to show them what they truly deserved was to set a precedent and be that change. Instead of sitting there telling them what was wrong with these young men, I decided to show them what right looked like. It changed my life. It benefited me as much as them. Without them, I may have never really realized how much I needed to change for the woman of my dreams. If I treated her like the queen she deserved, then maybe that would be what they needed to see to hold these men to the same standard. I can never change my past, I've yet to find the magic eraser to take away all the moments I regret, but I will never give up on my future.

The women of my family have always brought us so much happiness. The way Papi treated Nani, his daughter and his granddaughters set a standard that I lost sight of for a long time. As much as my family holds true to its core values, I began to find myself complacent. The reason families teach their kids certain morals and values isn't to just hold them true within the family dynamics itself but to apply it to the world around us. These three women reminded me just that. Without them, there is no telling if I ever would have truly realized how hypocritical I was. Lead by example is essential in good leadership in the military, but home life as well. When the day comes that I marry the woman of my dreams, and if I'm blessed with daughters, nieces, and grandkids of my own, I pray they look to me and my future wife for the standard like I looked to Nani and Papi. There is no such thing as a perfect guy, there's no secret template to tell guys how to act either, but when I spent all these years telling my three beautiful cousins what they deserved...I gave myself the base to build the best man I can be.

Every day I look in the mirror when I wake up and go to sleep. There will never be a day when I am content with the man in the mirror. I will continue to make my mistakes, but I've grown to learn from my mistakes, to give them a purpose. Be proud of who you are, but strive to be better. The success I have found in my relationships with friends and family has grown because of that. There will always be struggles and hurdles, but that's what makes people stronger. The desire to continue to grow doesn't mean you're not happy with yourself, it solely means you strive to make yourself better and those around you too. When the day comes I can marry the woman of my dreams, that mindset will hopefully be the core of our relationship because the moment your "ok" with where you are and who you are, is the day you begin to go backward versus forwards. I can thank my cousins for that.

The Bachelor Pad

My Uncle Carl taught me the true definition of tough love. There was no doubt he was the brother of my father, as similar as they were, yet they tipped opposite ends of the spectrum. Carl owns a construction Company and my father is a construction attorney. My father is capable of a little more "tact" in his approach, key word being capable, where Carl is a bit more direct. They were the dynamic duo together: and I don't think I've gone anywhere in the state of Ohio without someone knowing one of them. Carl's house had been a frequent visit for me from childhood until present, and after his divorce, it became referred to as the "Bachelor Pad."

Carl's house was like a resort: I'm not sure if it was the nerf gun arsenal in the basement, or that the only vehicles he owned were muscle cars and trucks. Carl's son Anthony was my brother Nick's age, and was home from Washington Jefferson college for one of the toughest summers I've had. He played football there and could bench press the weight equivalent of a train. CJ was in elementary school and had his black belt in karate nearly before he could speak, and could do about 95 pushups by the age of 6. They have their own horses, and probably the most well trained dogs I've ever seen (except Boomer). From anywhere in their house you can tell the dogs to "get behind the green line" and they go sit with their toes on the line of where the green carpet in the living room meets the kitchen tile. Their house is built on discipline, maturity, hard work, but family is its core. The responsibility I learned in this house is unprecedented. Anthony and CJ were like brothers to me, and Carl treated me like a son.

There are two pivotal moments in my life that I cannot imagine passing without their help. The first being my freshman year of high school right after I got to play my first football game. It was a mud pit (the best kind) and we were playing Cleveland Central Catholic which was arguably the worst team in our conference. Their skill level is probably the reason why I got a chance to play, and I played my heart out. I honestly had one the most memorable games of my sporting career. I had been begging God to show me some brief happiness because of my struggles at home, and finally here it was. I must have put some serious emphasis on "brief happiness" in my prayers because shortly after the game, I was informed I would be academically ineligible and unable play the remainder of the season. My heart dropped because I could picture in my head the anger and frustration that my father would feel. I was a dead man walking and obviously, in my own eyes, my academic ineligibility was everyone's fault but my own.

I had come up with this magnificent plan to call my mother to pick me up, and I would tell her on the way home praying she would just wind up telling dad. It had to be a miracle. When I called, she told me my cousin Anthony would be taking me back to his house and I would spend the night there. I didn't even begin to ask questions because I dodged a bullet. It gave me another 24 hours to find a way to break the news to my parents.

Carl's house was maybe 10 minutes away from Notre Dame Cathedral Latin (NDCL), but before we got there, I could tell something was off. Anthony had asked me if I wanted to pick up pizza on the way home, which was far from normal. Carl always had food at the house, and if he didn't, we always sat there and ordered pizza together. I *never* got to choose the pizza by myself.

The puzzle pieces came together when Carl sat me down and explained why I was there. He told me my brother Nick was being sent to a treatment facility in the Carolinas. My parents did everything they could to get Nick the best possible help across the country. Nick didn't know he was leaving, and there was much expected resistance when the people responsible for picking him up arrived in the middle of the night so my parents thought it would be best I stay at Carl's. I honestly don't think my Uncle Carl and cousins have any idea what they did for me through some of the toughest times I had with Nick. This wasn't the first time they would provide me a place of peace and serenity, and it definitely wasn't the last.

Carl is not the type of man who would just let me do whatever I wanted because I was going through tough times at home. If he had, I may not have made it out of them. Anthony, CJ and I became very close. Carl treated me like a son and taught me a lot about what it means to be a man. He called me on my self-pity and on my bad grades. He was tough on me like he was on his own boys, and I owe him the world for that. One night at dinner, while he was by the oven pulling out the pizza he had cooked for us, he asked me if I wanted some water with dinner. As I sat at the table I responded yes, and he fired back: "Well get off your ass and go get it; I'm not your waiter!"

I can imagine you could wonder what the significance of such a snappy remark could be. Carl gave me a key to his house, the code to his home alarm, and access to anything I may need, at any time. This came at a cost: I had to earn my place and in return he wouldn't treat me like a visitor. I took care of the horses, helped in the yard, helped stack the hay, cleaned the house, and I could stay there for weeks on end. This went on for years well after Nick returned. I didn't just go there when things were bad. All three of them became some of my greatest friends. CJ and I could play football in the basement for hours. Anthony invited me to go on vacation with him and two of his friends. It was the best time of my life.

We didn't talk much about my home life when I went there, but I knew if need be they were there to listen. Carl helped me get my first job down the street from his house bailing hay my sophomore year of high school. The farm was less than a mile from their house: I made great money, and it was tough work. Almost every night that summer I would stay at the Bachelor Pad and I worked there for the next two summers. I had the time of my life: I worked all day outside and then I would go spend the night with three of my best friends.

The second time they saved my life was that year on the Fourth of July when Nick and I had the fight of the century. It cut to my core when Nick and I fought because, as the years went on, I began to see the pain it brought my family. So often in my life when Nick and I fought all I could see was the impact it had on my own life. I felt that I was the victim, but it takes two to fight. When the police showed up at my house once again, I knew I had to leave. My entire family was gathering at Carl's house to celebrate the fourth and it didn't take a rocket scientist to gather that my immediate family would not be attending after this "incident". Nick wasn't going to leave, so that meant I was. This was the fight I talked about in Nick's chapter.

This wasn't the first time my family would be missing a family party because of Nick and my "brotherly love." I went to Carl's knowing upon my appearance they wouldn't even ask where my family was. It was already understood. Carl has this nice pool in his deck out back where the family was gathered eating when I arrived. This is when Carl and his tough love gave me a huge wakeup call. I walked around back with my head down and a couple bumps and bruises. Assuming if I acted like a victim, I wouldn't have to take responsibility for what happened. Once again, I would just blame it on Nick. I'll never forget what Carl told me when I turned that corner. "Stop dragging your head, it's just as much your fault as his. You don't always get a chance to explain your side, and there's no one here who has time to feel sorry for you. So, if you don't like the road you're on, then take a turn to a new one because no one will do it for you."

I hadn't even said my hellos yet and Carl had already called my bluff for pity. As blunt as it was, when I went home next is when I wrote Nick that letter asking to move forward. So, I owe that one to Carl.

Carl, CJ and Anthony took me in when I was in need, but if it wasn't for them and their tough love, I may still be drowning in my own self-pity. Seeing the way Anthony took care of his brother is what made me realize how much both of my brothers needed me to stand up and stand strong. The way Carl took care of me is something I will never be able to repay, but I will spend my whole life trying. These men are way more than family to me. They are my heroes. They are some of the hardest workers I have ever met. I will forever remember the summers we spent together and the many more to come.

Uncle Carl, you have raised two very incredible men. You should be beyond proud, and forever remember that you are not only a huge reason why I enlisted, but an even bigger reason I am the man I am today.

Anthony, the way you took care of me and brought me in with your friends changed my life. I've looked up to you my whole life. You were always so mature and had the coolest toys. Sorry for any of those I may/may not have broken.

CJ, I'm sorry for all the rug burns from carpet football, and for starting fights at your junior hockey games in the stands. I promise they were with good intentions.... but you and I have been great friends my entire life. From video games to football, whatever it was - you and I were always on the same team, which is probably why nobody ever wanted to play against us. We make a hell of a team, and I am very proud of the man you are growing to be.

The Squad Leader

It probably took me ten years of repeatedly asking my family how to spell my Aunt Lynnette's name before I decided to just chalk it up as a loss and call her "Lulu". I honestly couldn't tell you how that nickname started in our family. All I knew was it made my life a hell of a lot easier. Lulu is by far my biggest fan, and I am hers. My parents chose her and my Uncle Greg to be my Godparents, and ever since that day, she has signed everything she has ever sent me "your Fairy Godmother, Lulu". This includes the letters I got in basic training. Just imagine how that went over when the drill sergeants read those.

Lulu is my dad and Uncle Carl's sister. She is the oldest but by far the most spoiled by them. She is the princess of the family. I told you how close her son Matt and I are, and as much as she loves that, Matt was destined for medical school and I went a different direction with the Army. As much as Lulu loved hosting the sleepovers with Matt and I when we were younger, there was one condition that I couldn't escape. It was mandatory that before I came in the house, I must take off my shoes and get frisked for weapons and every time without fail she would find Nerf guns, play swords, hand cuffs. You name it, and I probably had it. While Matt was doing his homework, I was practicing G.I. Joe combat maneuvers in the living room, normally breaking things. As much as I joke around, the day I joined the Army, Lulu became my biggest fan.

Lulu is probably 5'0 in heels. She's a petite Italian woman who is as pretty as they come. Let me tell you, Lulu has the beauty and the brains. She is a prime example of great things come in small packages. She is a Certified Nurse Practitioner at the Cleveland Clinic and is definitely where Matt got his medical calling. I could spend every single day with Lulu, she is the type of woman that makes every day just that much better. This is the same woman who bought our entire family matching shirts for Christmas that say "squad" on the chest, hence her self-appointed position of "Squad Leader". I wouldn't trade Lulu for the world.

What has amazed me about Lulu for years is her ability to care for every single patient like it was her only one. As cliché as that may sound, just imagine if the whole world treated each person they encountered like they were the only person around. I know I speak for myself when I say when I face struggles throughout my life, there are times I feel engulfed in them. Like quicksand, I just can't seem to get ahead but then out of nowhere comes someone like Lulu. As small as she may seem, her strength is unbelievable. Regardless what hardships she found herself in, somehow, someway, she pushes it all to the side to help others.

The first day after I was discharged, I went to surprise Lulu at work. I told this gentleman behind the counter I didn't want to disrupt any of her patients or schedule. Not a minute later she comes power walking around the corner and nearly tackled me to the ground with a hug. She took me around her office and introduced me to *every single person* that worked in her office. I believe her intentions were to show how proud she was of me; but when I left I was even more proud of her. We are each other's biggest fan. She had her own flag pole in her yard, and yellow ribbons around her trees until the day I came home. When she walked me around that day, I was more proud of her then she could ever be of me. The way people look at her, and the way people talk to her, is more than any nephew could ask for. She is as humble as they come. These men and women in her office tell me how incredible my aunt is because of how she treats everyone. They absolutely adore her.

The summer when I came home from overseas with my injury I could barely walk. Lulu jumped through every hoop and hurdle she could to get me to see the doctors I needed. I was so humbled to see all these people willing to help me, but more importantly, the way they helped her. Military insurance is tricky when you are home on leave. My father was kind enough to help me pay for these appointments without worrying if he would be reimbursed. We spent countless hours working with the kind finance lady at the Cleveland Clinic. I told her time and time again how indebted to her I was, and one time she stopped me. "Before you thank me again, just know there is never enough I could do for your family." As appreciative as I was I didn't understand what she meant. I love my family and all, but this lady came in early, and worked late every day for a week just to help me with paperwork. She turned to my father and I with a tear in her eye and said: "Your Aunt saved my husband's life. She was the only one who caught what was wrong with him, and saved his life; if it wasn't for her my husband wouldn't be here." Lulu had never told any of our family about this. She is as humble as they come, which is what makes her so breath taking.

She brings people cake and cookies for birthdays. She knows the names of her patient's kids. In a world where repetition could easily bring complacency, she has prevailed in a way that gives me chills. We all know you don't do kind things expecting a reward. Lulu does what she does because that's how her heart works. That's how she chooses to live each day. She is passionate about what she does, and as repetitive and busy as her schedule gets, she treats every single patient like they are the only person in the world. That type of attention is what saved that man's life, and in turn maybe saved my spine and ability to walk. If that lady hadn't helped me the way she did, there is no telling if I would ever walk normally again. It's amazing the miracles that happen when you treat people the way God intended for every human to be treated. I brag about Lulu every day because as tough as the times were when I was away, all I could imagine is Lulu at work making these people's lives better. The day I left the military I was presented a plaque, with text containing a bible verse. A bible verse that my leadership thought fit me, and if that is true, it is only because I learned it from Lulu. *"But he knows the way I take; when he has tested me, I will come forth as gold"* Job 23:10. Every day we face issues of our own. It takes someone with an impenetrable heart and strength to put others needs above their own. In a world where our society builds these perfect stereotypes, we begin to compare ourselves to

77

others around us, and judge. Stay humble and show humility.

Hard work is essential in every single aspect of my family. My grandparents instilled it in their three children who are beyond successful at what they do. As essential as that characteristic is to find success in life, there's another which defines Lulu. Compassion. Lulu taught me something I will never forget. On a day when I was at her house, I was talking about my brother Nick out of frustration in a disrespectful way. Lulu heard me. She yelled at me like you couldn't imagine. As small as she is, she has the roar of a lion. She definitely is Nani's daughter. She told me "You know you aren't any better than your brother. Get off your high horse Timmy, because as great as you think you are, there is always someone better."

She was dead on. The low self-esteem I had for myself growing up, combined with that pent-up anger, really did create this self-made pedestal. I was so quick to put Nick down because I thought it was what people wanted to hear. My family called me out on a lot of my mistakes when I was young, and I am forever indebted to them for that. Lulu was right; you're not better than others. Sometimes we find ourselves in a better situation than someone else, but that doesn't make us better. Whether it's financially, emotionally, spiritually, whatever, if you find yourself in a better position than someone, humble yourself and help raise them up. I can only imagine where I would be today if my family and friends left me in the dust because I was slowing them down. Lulu learned that from Papi. Papi treated the man who cleaned his restroom in his assisted living place the same way he treated the owner. Just because you make more money than someone, or have a bigger house, maybe even nicer clothes or a car, doesn't mean you are any better. Stay humble, and have compassion. Everyone has their dark days whether they want to admit it or not. Everyone has been knocked down and stuck their hand up looking and praying someone would help them to get back up on their feet. Compassion: It's as vital as oxygen, and we can have an endless supply if we choose to.

Good Ol' Gregor

There is one thing I brace myself for every time we have a family party, and that would be the "hug" I get from my Uncle Greg. The reason I put "hug" in quotations is because it toes the line between a hug and feeling like you were crushed in a car compactor. A few days after my first back surgery we were heading over to see some family where of course Greg would be, and the entire twenty-minute drive all I imagine was him picking me up and crushing me with his hug. You can imagine the implications that could have. I made my rounds greeting everyone, and before you know it here comes Greg and I'm not positive, but I'm pretty sure I heard the Jaws theme song as he began his approach. He walked right past me, "Hey Timmy (my entire family calls me Timmy)" grazed his hand over my shoulder and went right on by.

I promise there is a reason for me telling you that story. I have already told you about my cousin Matt and Mikey. Uncle Greg is their father just to help you connect the dots. Greg is one who loves his space, like me. So often when I would come home on leave, and understandably so, I would try to cram spending as much time with everyone I could but a few weeks is never enough time. The first few days were crazy, and naturally the first few times I saw everyone the greetings were much more complicated than the traditional hello. I could count on Greg for more than his gorilla hugs. When the commotion got crazy, and I finally had a moment to myself, I would make my way to some corner of the room and there would be Greg. We both like to make sure everyone is enjoying themselves, but when it's our turn to enjoy ourselves, sitting in the chair in the corner is just perfect. Some of the best conversations I had with my uncle are in these moments of solitude and peace. He was always the last person to welcome me home, and as crazy as it sounds I couldn't thank him enough for that. He knew that I knew, when I found the time I would come find him. The few days after my surgery were no different.

I am as stubborn as it gets at times, and I'm sure the majority of you reading this have found times in your life when all you want to do is just be alone. Not because anything is wrong or that your upset with anyone, but there is a certain sense of serenity you feel when your able to just shut everything out. The first two years of my short Army career were overseas. Twelve countries, and when I came home on leave, all I wanted to do was just be at peace. Family and friends brought me that peace. Not going to clubs or bars as most twenty some year old's may enjoy. Family parties and breakfast at Nani and Papi and the whole family are what made those few days home seem like an eternity. I would be lying though if I said I didn't get smothered. I would never complain about getting attention from family, and it's nobody's fault, but it was a relief when story time was over and I had a moment of peace. It never failed, when I finally made my way to the quietest room in the house, there was Greg.

Even before the military, Greg was the only one who never asked me what my plans were. He was the only one I knew I didn't need to have some elaborate presentation created for what the next decade of my life looked like. Parents always ask what you're going to study, what your grades look like. Grandma and Grandpa want to know about girlfriends, jobs, savings accounts. I love my family, and most of you can relate to this, but these questions are taxing. And as I mentioned before, I was failing my classes. I had no clue what I wanted to study, so as intimidating as the spot light is when you're passing your classes, just imagine how I felt with nothing to show for myself.

I worked for Greg for two long summers at his Garden Center. He kept me busy, gave me an opportunity to make great money for a summer job in college, but most importantly he taught me to enjoy life. I never needed answers when around Greg. Working at the Garden Center was pretty straight forward. You clocked in and Greg told us what job we had to do that day. He didn't tell us what he had scheduled six weeks out: He focused on that day and that day only. As simple as it was, I began to apply that to my life. Instead of overwhelming myself with trying to have all the answers for the future, I gained control of one day at a time. Obviously, the Garden Center had more work scheduled then just one day out, but Greg knew that as we began to manage more effectively he would challenge us with more. I applied that same concept to myself. It would be ignorant of me to say "I live my life one day at a time" because life does require some planning. But without being able to seize the day I was in, there was no hope for me to effectively navigate the days which followed.

This mentality followed me into the next fall, which is when I enlisted. Even school was different. That semester I earned the best grades I had in years. The simple mindset Greg showed me became the structure I build my life around today. It was a huge reason why I chose to enlist as well. I knew that if I didn't take the few moments to speak with the recruiter, or even came up with some excuse why I couldn't make it into his office. I may have never fulfilled my dream.

My heart was filled with a passionate desire to serve in the Army. The calling was so intense that, without taking it just one day at a time, it may have become so overwhelming that it would end up just like another opportunity I let slip through my fingertips. An opportunity to show the world who Tim Natale really was. I spoke with the recruiter on campus, and the next day I went to his office. A few days following, I was signing the dotted line which was by far the most stressful choice of my life. I made it through thanks to Greg.

It was nice to share that desire for solitude with someone like Greg, and the ability to enjoy each day. Obviously, in the military there is no promise of tomorrow. Even in the civilian world, there's no guarantee that tomorrow will come around. So often in our lives we feel like things are running a million miles an hour and it's hard to sit down and just take a moment. So much of my life has been filled with stresses, and the military understandably added to that. Moments like those are when Greg has taught me so much. He is a man of few words, but my father always told me "less is more." Greg and I would sit and have some of the simplest conversations, so simple in fact to him that's all they may have been. Just a conversation. During these conversations, life seemed to slow down, almost as if time stopped. He really taught me to enjoy every moment you have; life is definitely a blessing. My days on leave went so fast, and some of the best moments I had were those conversations with Greg. Time slowed just enough where he would remind me of just how fortunate we all were to be together. Some of Greg's finest words to me were intended to be a joke. When I told, him it sucked I only had 16 days to be home and he responded: "Well enjoy what you were blessed with, because it could have been only 15."

Federal Escort

I was never the best football player, so you can probably guess why I was so nervous going to Gettysburg football camp my freshman year. I hadn't met anyone in high school yet because it was still summer, and I had to get on this bus and spend a few weeks with people I didn't know playing a sport I wasn't all that good at. I'm not two steps on the bus before realizing there are no free seats. The only seat that looks to have the slightest potential is filled with the kid's lunch boxes, and I say lunch boxes because there must have been 7 or 8.

"Come on man take a seat, you can just set those any-where man, most of them are empty already anyway." How could one kid finish three or four full sized lunch boxes be-fore the bus has even taken off you ask, well let me intro-duce Michael Hayslip.

Michael and I spent the next four years of high school studying hard, and ended up graduating number 1 and 2 of our class in 2010. Okay, so that may not be entirely true, but it's all about the effort, right? I can assure you that every teacher knew who we were, and there was a good chance we did graduate number 1 and 2 if detention had a graduation ceremony. Mike was the only person that my mother let stay over during the school week and that has a lot to do with the fact we didn't get home from detention until 7 or 8 at night. It doesn't make much sense to separate the two of us at that point anyway, so carpooling to detention became a reality.

Michael and I were not bad kids; we just liked to have our fun. If you found one of us, the other was there somewhere. We spent so much time together I actually started calling Mrs. Hayslip, well, "Mom." He started to go to my house when I wasn't even home and still does to this day. My parents call Michael another son, and he is probably the favorite. Mike is the first of five of my friends I'd like to introduce you to that my family has pretty much adopted over the years.

When it was time for college, Mike picked Toledo. I could care less about college at the point, so what could be better than going to Toledo as well. Mike had even come to work bailing hay with me the summer before college, so I mean it when I say we were always together. Mike and I had the time of our lives, but like I mentioned before, I had my fair share of rough patches. Hanging out with Mike was a way for me to take my mind of those struggles. In high school, I dreaded coming home, but when Mike came with me, it was different. Mike is the one who got me into working out, which was a savior of a stress reliever for so many years. There is something about Mike that made him different from a lot of kids my age. Like I said, Mike and I were not "scholars" in the traditional sense, but when it came to athletics, I'm convinced he was made in a lab. If there is such thing as God given talent, Michael had it, and a lot of it. What made him different was his will.

Freshman year he injured his shoulder in a football game. When I say injured I mean dislocated so badly his hand could touch his knee. Our athletic trainer was adamant that Michael would not be finishing the game. He laid Michael down and reset his shoulder. Michael pleaded for his life to reenter the game, so the compromise was 'if you can do a pushup you can go back in'. Michael did a pushup, with one arm. You could see the pain, but the reason I'm telling you this is not because I want to preach to you about Michael's toughness but rather his die-hard refusal to accept defeat until he knew he had nothing left.

So often in my life I quit once I hit resistance for the first time. I found myself in a rhythm and finding success, and when I hit a barrier or resistance I would quit. School, sports, yard work with dad - it didn't matter. Here is Michael who had made up his mind that when the day comes where football is no longer an option for him, Mike would be at peace knowing he put his heart and soul into it. All of it, every step. He would never look back and wonder if he had given it his entire heart and soul. That dedication combined with his talent was an awesome combination.

Looking back, that specific instance wasn't the best idea from a medical standpoint, but there's not an amount of money in the world that could keep him from football. It was his outlet: his passion, and he poured his heart and soul into it. Sometimes we let people tell us what we are able to do, what we probably will fail at, and when it's time to hang it up and move on. Not Mike. We have a tendency to let people set limits for us and we let them hinder our dreams and cap our potential. We let people tell us what we are and are not capable of, but not Mike. Mike has been hurt time and time again. Knee and shoulder surgeries in the four short years of high school. Every single time, he suited up again and held nothing back. I will never forget what he told me when I asked him if he had thought about quitting football. He said "It's not just about football itself; it's about loving what you do. There's not a person on this earth that will tell me when it's time to stop other than myself or God."

I may not be able to speak for everyone, but I know that there are so many instances in my life where I met resistance and I quickly considered the idea that maybe I should just reroute and try something else which is exactly what I did time and time again. Whether it was changing majors in college, or sports, workout routines, etc. It took me so long to truly realize how some of the toughest fights we have in life are truly worth the effort in the long run. If you stick it out through the first couple of hurdles, it begins to become more manageable and the feeling of accomplishment is unprecedented when you accomplish something that which at one point seemed impossible.

Mike is a huge reason why I joined the Army. He showed me when you know you want something, love something, need something, the only way to lose it is to let it go. The Army is what I wanted and what I needed. Without Mike, I may have let it go and settled for what society dictated my life to be, not what I wanted my life to be.

Mike wasn't just a stud athlete and good friend; he was a support beam for my life. He stood by me when I didn't even stand by myself. He helped me up when I got knocked down, time and time again. He brushed me off and said 'you're okay'. Over a decade later Mike and I still act like we did in high school. We haven't grown up much, we still do our fair share of dumb things, but I trust Mike with my life. Ten years later and he still stands right by my side in some of the toughest moments of my life, and ten years later he is definitely responsible for some of the best moments of my life as well.

I will never forget the days of Papi's wake and funeral. As sad as those days were for me, there were some moments which I knew even made Papi smile. Michael Hayslip, the first kid I met in high school, a decade later continues to find ways to make some of the toughest days bearable for me. He showed up to my grandfather's wake and walks straight up to me and asks me if there is food there. He didn't do it to make me laugh. He was dead serious. Michael was at the wake from start to finish, and even his family showed up. It wasn't until the funeral when my emotions started to get the best of me. My cousin Matt wrote an incredible Eulogy, and whoever picked the music was definitely trying to make people cry. I will never forget sitting in the Mass trying to just stay settled, when I look back and see Mike waving. Mike is sitting in the crowd waving at me like he didn't know I would be there. My dad calls Mike and I "dumb and dumber" and moments like these support those nick names.

The Mass ended and I was walking Papi's casket out with my brothers and cousins. I greeted a few people, and opened the passenger seat door for Kelsey Rose, when Mike comes flying over the backseat. He drove his own car, and I'm convinced he rode with me because he was too lazy to put gas in it. But I couldn't have been happier he rode with us. We are about halfway to the cemetery in the funeral procession when we approach another routine traffic light. The FUNERAL escort car pulled into the left lane to block oncoming traffic, and we proceed to turn left. Mind you, the top is off of my Wrangler, and Michael is standing up holding onto the roll cage in my grandfather's funeral procession. If you know Michael, you will know that he and I together we are not the brightest bulbs you'll ever encounter.

Mike takes one look at the escort car, points his two fingers at the car like they are old western revolvers, and yells "federal escort" like we were being escorted by the secret service. I had been dating Kelsey Rose for about four and a half years at this point, but had never seen her laugh as hard as she did at that moment. We both had tears in our eyes from laughing, and without Michael realizing it, he had shown me that this day didn't have to be sad and miserable. It was right on que, as if Papi had Mike on strings trying to cheer me up.

Mike and I acted like brothers from the start, but since I joined the military, it's been different. Mike and I both grew up, sort of. I come home on leave, and Mike comes over like its high school all over again. It's not like I was gone for a year, but more like 20 minutes. It's not some big greeting and talking about how much we've both done since we last saw each other. He doesn't ask to come over, or what I'm doing. He just shows up. I could be gone for a year and Mike will walk in the house without anyone being home, and be eating food on the couch watching TV like he lives there. That what makes Mike, Mike. He is terrible at giving me advice when I am struggling, and he cannot have a serious conversation to save his life; but Mike has pulled me out of some very dark places just being himself. He showed me that you don't always need to say the right words, and do the right thing, to help someone. You don't need to try to be someone you're not to be there for someone. It's not always about having the right things to say, it's about being genuine in someone's time of need. When I sat down to write this book, and I started to think about some of the tougher times I've had since high school, Mike was there every time.

One of the toughest 24 hours of my life was the night I found out my friend was killed. I felt overwhelmed with pain, to the point I just wanted to spend the night alone. I had an early MRI in the morning for my back, which ultimately decided my fate in the military, and I was just sitting there feeling sorry for myself. Kelsey Rose had gone home and all of a sudden, some car pulled into the driveway. You know its Mike because he's the only one who locks his car at my house, which is in the middle of the woods. He gave no warning he's coming over, he just made that choice on his own like normal. I hadn't told him my friend had been killed, so he just comes up to the loft where I'm sitting, turns on the video game, and hands me a controller. He notices I'm a little down and when he asks what wrong I just simply said it had been a rough day with which he replies "Well you're still alive aren't you?" He's not even looking at me when he said it. In fact, it was kind of under his breath, but he was right.

Mike didn't say it because he was reminding me I was still alive even if a dear friend of mine was gone. How could he, he didn't know my friend had been killed. Mike had unintentionally said the words I needed to hear to pick myself up. I doubt Michael even remembers saying those words. Something so simple from Mike just being Mike, hit home for me. It didn't require him to think of the right advice. He didn't even know what was wrong, but somehow, he found a way to make it alright.

I am a firm believer God gives his toughest battles to his strongest soldiers. Maybe I just bought into that when I was younger to validate why I kept encountering struggles. Most of us find ourselves in a moment where we start to find happiness and peace like I did that night with Mike, and then all of a sudden here comes a curveball. That curveball came to me at about 4 a.m. when Mike and I were still up playing video games. It came in the sound of my phone ringing, which is never a good sign at that hour in the night. It was my little brother Dom calling me from jail telling me he had been arrested. He had gotten in trouble with his friends for knocking over a mailbox. His "friends" had left him there to take the fall. Whether this was the truth or not, I had one hour to get to the police station on Mayfield Road with the $700 bail. Could this day get any worse?

I get off the phone and Mike is just looking at me like he had it all figured out. He had been around the Natale house for roughly a decade at this point. So, he had pretty good idea of what it would take if we were going to pull this off without waking up dad. He formulated a plan which took that into account; got us to Mayfield Road (which was roughly a 35-minute drive) and allows Mike to get a snack while heading out the door, all within the allotted time frame. Needless to say, the plan failed terribly. My dad woke up immediately to Michael grabbing enough food from the kitchen for a hibernating bear.

That night could not have been any more stressful, but Mike was there every step of the way. I had just briefly explained to him that my friend had been killed on our trip. He could have gone home considering the police station was about 3 minutes from his house, but he didn't. He even yelled at my brother before I did. Mike didn't give Dom a lecture, and once again he didn't have the right things to say. But Mike had found a way to help my family without even realizing it. I can't count how many times in my life I have put off helping a friend of mine for some selfish reason; but without fail, Mike dropped everything he was doing countless times to help me and my family.

Michael helped me survive one of the worst nights of my life without changing a single step from his normal activities. When I got home from the MRI without a wink of sleep yet, he was still at my house. He was still playing video games, but somehow that made the news of a career-ending injury a little less damaging. Mike was just Mike, but without him, God only knows how some of the toughest moments in my life would have ended.

My dad tells me that Mike and I are twins. I am not a pretty boy like Mike, so my father must be referring to our personalities. Mike will spend days or even weeks at a time at my house. Whether it was high school, when I was home on leave from the Army, or now that I'm home for good, Mike and I are always together. Mike and I have had our fair share of questionable moments, but I can guarantee if you need a laugh, even two minutes with us will do the trick.

We have had our laughs, and we have caused our fair share of chaos in this world. When it comes down to it, there is a reason my Papi could remember Mike's name as he began to slip into confusion. He could see the impact Mike had on my life. Nobody can ever convince me that your brothers have to be blood.

Mike, words can't describe my appreciation for your brotherhood over the years. It was no coincidence that God had you by my side in my darker days, and there is no doubt in my mind that's the same reason you feel the same calling towards the military. Just know, wherever the world takes you, God has a plan for you my friend. Papi told me something the day I handed him an award I received after my tour. He told me: "be proud of the man you have become, don't ever forget the people who helped you get there."

Ry Guy

The first memory I have of my friend Ryan Walzcak was in the second grade; he tripped over a lunch box and fell the three steps outside of St. Rita Elementary School, and ruptured his spleen. Luckily, he made a full recovery, but I mean a lunch box...really? Needless to say, he found his balance and footing in life; he is currently in medical school, and even though he is a Pittsburg Steelers fan, he and I have remained good friends over the years. Ryan was the type of guy who you couldn't spend more than five minutes with without him making you laugh so hard you almost wet yourself. He doesn't even try to be funny, and I think that's what makes it as great as it is. Ryan and I went to grade school and most of high school together. Right around seventh grade, he went back to Pennsylvania for a year or two, then came to Notre Dame Cathedral Latin for high school. He and I became good friends during our time together at NDCL. Ryan may have been the class clown, but he was also the smart kid who could forget that exam week was coming up, wake up and ace all his finals like it was nothing.

Mike Hayslip may have been the first person I met in high school, but Ry Guy was my roommate at the Gettysburg football camp, and I knew him from elementary school. By the time were had returned from camp, I had a pretty good group of friends. Ryan had introduced me to his friend Shane Voyles, who becomes more a part of the story in just a little bit. Ryan's older brother drove me home from football every day that fall. The first day I brought all my buddies to my house, I laid out some ground rules. My dad is very particular about his house, and rightfully so, he had worked hard to make it all it was. My dad was beyond welcoming to my friends, as long as they respected his rules: 1. take care of his things, clean up after yourself, and don't break anything; 2. NO DRINKING and this rule I was terrified to break, and trust me so were they.

The first day they all met my dad we were all hanging out in the basement, and my dad couldn't figure out to turn his TV on...this still happens to this very day, you just make this stuff up. We were making quite a bit of noise, and my dad came down. All we could think is, "Oh crap, we woke him up!" He looks at us with this blank stare like he was going to kill us all. Tired, stressed, my dad is just standing there looking at us; after what seemed like an eternity of silence he says "Which one of you F*****s is going to get my TV to turn on?"

Ry Guy to the rescue. Nearly a decade later we still talk about that night like it was yesterday. I have mentioned it before, but high school had some very tough times for me, and if it wasn't for my group of friends, I have no clue where I would be. Each person in our group had their role, and I would like to think other than Ry guy being the smart one, he was also the one that could get us out of any trouble. Whatever dumb stuff we did, if we blamed it on Ry Guy the teachers would just shake their heads and drop it. Shane, Mike and I probably had enough detentions for our entire grade, but Ry Guy could have gotten away with murder. Shane was smart too, but Ry Guy is the type of smart that almost makes you mad.

There were days I dreaded going to school, but somehow regardless how bad the night before may have been at home, my friends found a way to distract me. Ry Guy's humor played a huge part in that. Everyone loves Ryan. I could say something in class, and I'm getting detention: Ry Guy could say the same thing and the teachers would be laughing. It was nice not to have to talk about why I was struggling, especially being a high school guy, I didn't want to talk about my problems, but it's different not to have too. To have friends like Ryan who know your struggling, but they just find a way to take your mind off of it.

There is one day which I genuinely can never repay Ryan for. My mom had rented this game for the Wii called *Wii Recess* and the only reason I liked it was because it had dodgeball. Obviously, I needed to bring this epic game to my friends. It would change the way they see the world. This was a game for the century, and I was the one delivering the holy grail. My brother Dom and I had been playing it for weeks, so long, in fact, we had tallied up roughly $30 in late fees from Blockbuster. My mother was the bearer of bad news when she informed us all that this was the last night with the game, in her frustration, she would be returning it the next day. This was the last possible night to show my friends who were all patiently waiting at Ry Guy's house for the game of the century.

Anyone with siblings, especially brothers, knows this type of news is all it takes for World War III to break out. My brother Nick didn't even like playing it, but he refused to let me take it for no other reason than not letting me take it. There is no explanation, but my parents can attest that this type of argument, in fact, was all too common between him and I. Fighting essentially just to fight. Fight we did, so bad in fact that my mother told me, in a moment of desperation, to leave and not to come back. I couldn't explain the rage and frustration that I had while driving to Ryan's. I can tell you that I had no intention of returning. I just remember sitting in my Toyota Highlander trying to cool off before walking in his house, so my mood didn't have to ruin a fun night with friends. Only to find that fight had taken too long that by the time I arrived at Ryan's he was the only one left. The Holy Grail in hand, him having no idea what it cost me to get it there, Shane and Mike had gone home.

What had happened between Nick and I was the last straw. I had told myself so many times before; I'm done, but for some reason this was it. I wasn't planning on going home. Ryan and I played Wii dodgeball until the sun came up the next morning. I am not lying, not a wink of sleep. I had the time of my life, though; we had a blast. He is a smart kid, I highly doubt he couldn't sense my anger or frustration when I arrived, but he didn't ask. Maybe he just knew I would tell him if I wanted to.

I genuinely don't know, but it does speak to the impact Ry Guy had on my life during some of the toughest years of it. He may not even remember because maybe to him it was just playing video games, an epic game at that. He had made such an impact that night; I drove home the next day without even remembering what had happened. It wasn't until the next night when my mom needed to take the game back, that I remembered the Battle Royale from the night before, but at this point, it didn't even matter.

Needless to say, the next weekend Shane and I drove to probably four or five different Blockbusters trying to find the game, and we found it. There were many more sleepless nights when Wii dodgeball was involved. When I was young I didn't want to talk to any of our family therapists, I didn't want to pour my struggles out to my buddies, I wanted to have a good time and indeed times like these I did. Ryan and I haven't talked a lot since high school. I would still see him when I was home on leave if he's back from medical school, and it's like we picked up right where we left off. I invited him to the Browns final game of the year in 2016. I was two weeks out of my first back surgery, and my cousin Matt and I had bought 15 tickets. Even though that traitor loves the Steelers, it just wouldn't be the same without Ry Guy. My dad always told me I had some of the greatest friends; it may be because Ryan fixed his TV that day, or maybe he saw the impact they had on me. Loyalty and genuine friendship is something our world finds at a scarcity, but it's not gone. I couldn't have asked for a better group of friends. If the tables were turned, it's hard to say I wouldn't have ran out of there the moment I met my family. It was like a mad house at home most days, but Ryan, and my buddies still stuck around. My father used to tell me "it's not about having a million friends; it's about having a few friends who stick with you from start to finish...and you can count your true friends in life on one hand."

SHANEO-V-HAS-TO-PEE

I was never musically inclined, and if I lined up all of my friends and asked you to pick out the one you think could play ACDC's Thunderstruck intro with his eyes closed, Shane Voyles would be the last one you would pick. Shane is a six-foot tall red head who gets sun burned so easily he could get scorched watching the weather channel. He can't even talk about sun!

Ryan introduced me to Shane in Gettysburg football camp before freshman year. At that time, AIM instant messenger was still "cool", and this guy's username was "Shaneovhastopee" which was, and still is, legendary.

I had known Ry Guy and spent the bus ride down getting to know Michael Hayslip. I had been nervous about high school, as I mentioned, and here I had three great friends before school even started.

Within my first few weeks of school, Nick was in bad shape. Not even two months in, he was sent away to the treatment program. I'm no psychologist, but I would imagine I'm not far from the truth saying the type of stress I dealt with so early in my life could have played an extremely negative and lasting impact on me if I let it. Without people like Shane, it might have.

It's probably no surprise to the majority of people reading this that high schoolers often experiment with alcohol.

I mentioned before that no alcohol was permitted in my house and from day one my friends respected my dad's rule. I owe a lot of that to Shane. Shane was the type of friend who took the lead. He would make the plans, and we would all just follow along. Shane would bring his friends from grade school to my house, and naturally the more people that arrived the more I feared alcohol would show up. I could care less what other kids did at their own houses, but I never had the urge to drink, and I definitely didn't have the urge strong enough to risk my dad finding out. Before I could finish my little speech about the ground rules to Shane's friends, I was always interrupted by someone saying "Yeah, Shane already told us, no worries."

There is a lot of pressure in high school, not just with drinking, but just to fit in, generally. This is no surprise, but on top of the fear someone would come into my house and break one of my dad's simple rules, I was terrified what might happen with Nick. Nick wanted nothing more than to fit in with my friends but it was never that easy for Nick. I was the smallest of my friends. If Nick decided to pick a fight with one of my friends, he was in for a surprise. As I mentioned, people listened to Shane, and Shane knew that. He wasn't arrogant, and that is honestly why, to this day, I respect him as much as I do. He was a big kid; an athletic and natural leader and that's why people respected his words. So, when Shane told someone the rules of my house, those rules were never broken.

Shane looked out for me a lot during school and is a huge reason why my life didn't turn into some crazy roller coaster. He kept me on track, and with him around, I never felt pressured to drink at parties or when we were out. I assume the majority of us have experienced peer pressure of "Come on; just have one drink". Shane was always the first one to come up and crush it. "He said he didn't want one." It may sound dumb to a high school kid at a party, but my extended family has a history of alcohol abuse. I was genuinely not interested in drinking, and I never even told Shane those details. He may have known that, with all the stress I had, and regardless of alcohol abuse in my extended family, alcohol wasn't a good solution to my problems. He never asked why I didn't drink. He never tried to push it on me. He accepted it and stood by my choices. Anyone who has been through similar scenarios knows how reassuring it can be when, without hesitation, someone stands by every choice you make.

There are two memorable times in my life when Shane showed his true colors. The first time was when I didn't make the baseball team my junior year. The second was the day my fears became reality when Nick picked a fight with Shane.

Baseball was my way of building a personal relationship with Papi from a very early age. He loved the game. Papi actually played for the Navy and the farm team for the New York Yankees. As much as I loved baseball, the day came when my career was cut short. My high school was notorious for its baseball teams, which was one of the reasons I chose to go there. My freshman and sophomore year I was on the team even though I didn't play much. Junior year however, I got cut. Honestly, this was the first time I had really faced individual failure; failure that was my fault and responsibility. I couldn't make excuses for what happened, or blame it on someone else, and it hit me hard. I never thought I would get cut. As humbling as it was, I was crushed to have to call Papi and tell him that there wouldn't be any more games for him to attend. All my friends were football players, except me. Like I said, I got hurt freshman year so that was cut short as well; so baseball gave me a little bit of identity among my friends. When I got cut, I expected to be given a hard time by my friends. That's just what high school boys do; they joke around with each other. You don't take it personally, it's all in good fun, but I knew this would be different. This was hitting me hard, and like I said, I hadn't met failure face to face like this. Regardless of everything my father had told me, I walked out of the meeting with the coaches with my head down. I walked right into Shane. He was great at guitar, football, and baseball. He was the catcher and actually played varsity as a sophomore the year prior. What made Shane, Shane was his genuinely humble attitude. He had so much to brag about but simply chose not to talk about himself. In fact, the day I got cut, Shane didn't make a single joke; he respected my pain. He knew what baseball meant to me because we played together those years prior. That day, Shane sat and talked to me for probably three hours. I kept saying "I failed" and what he told me has remained with me to this day. He told me "Failing is only when you decide you're not getting back up."

He wasn't talking about baseball; he meant in life. That is exactly what Papi told me too when I called him. Shane sat right there when I made that call to Papi. Shane could have been out celebrating the start of another great year of making one of the best baseball teams in the state, but he didn't. He was humble, and instead of leaving me in his dust – he helped me back up.

The second instance Shane showed his true colors is when one of my deepest fears came true. I was terrified when I brought friends home that Nick wouldn't get along with them and they wouldn't want to come back. More specifically, I feared that Nick would get violent with them like he and I were together. His mental disorders make those situations very difficult to predict and, unfortunately, they were not few and far between. Jokingly, one day, Nick decided to pick at Shane. As I have said before, Shane is not and was not ever a small man by any stretch of the word. Nick was just giving Shane a hard time, but it was getting to Shane. Nick just wanted to spend time with my friends, but the struggles between he and I made that nearly impossible without conflict. When I would tell Nick to back off after a while, things went south. I made my fair share of attempts to include Nick, but his social anxieties made it difficult for him to just tag along, and he would act out.

Shane had this ability to just brush off Nick's behavior, but you can imagine how taxing that must have been. Nick knew Shane wouldn't call him out, so he just kept poking the bear. The moment came when Nick's brain told him it would be a good idea to try to tackle Shane. All 140 lbs. of Nick came running at Shane from one end of our basement to the other. The "collision" consisted of Nick running into Shane, and without Shane even bracing, Nick hitting the floor like a bag of bricks. I was furious, embarrassed, enraged. Mind you, this isn't some 4-year-old terrorizing my friends, it was my older brother by nearly 2 years. Times like these made it very difficult for me to accept his struggles with mental disabilities and disorders. As I began to storm toward Nick for another brother on brother brawl, Shane put his hand up on my chest stopping me. Instead of acting out of anger or frustration like most others would after being barreled into, he sat down on the floor next to Nick.

He pulled up the video from his Facebook account that he had played for my friends and I moments earlier. Instinctively, Shane acted out of compassion for my brother, sat with him, and just gave him a few moments to relax. Just the few minutes Shane took to sit one-on-one with Nick, and that was all Nick wanted and needed - a friend. Months, sometimes even years, would go between visits from someone specifically for Nick. All he wanted was someone to hang out with like I had, and Shane gave him that. Shane wasn't a push over, and he didn't act out of pity, but he showed compassion and an unprecedented humble persona time and time again.

Without Shane's repeated acts, those stresses I talked about earlier may have gotten the best of me. Things with Nick were so tough, but moments like that day in the basement gave me just enough of a break to make it manageable and eventually gave me the ability to forgive. Countless times Shane has shown me the true meaning of humility and service to others. High school had some of the darkest times in my life, but I made through out because of people like Shane. Friendship isn't about the number of followers you have on some website or how many people like a picture you post; it's about the people who are by your side for the best and worst moments of your life, beginning to end. Together you fight the punches life throws you and celebrate each time you find success. You fight the punches life throws you, and celebrate each time you find success.

Made in America

I genuinely don't know why I started calling my friend Matt Dipasqua "the big man." If I had to guess, it would be because he was bigger than me, which isn't saying much because I think when we graduated high school I was 120 lbs. Whatever the reason it stuck. Matt and I didn't really become good friends until senior year. I never really thought about it. We had always been around the same people, but just randomly started hanging out one day, I guess. The end of senior year, Matt and I spent a lot of time together, and I doubt he realized it, but my house always kind of ran more smoothly when he was around. The summer before college I would come home from work and either his truck or Michael Hayslip's Jeep would be in my driveway...normally both. When I came home on leave from the Army, they were at my house on the couch before I even made it in the door. My dad still asks if "the big man" is coming over for dinner.

After my freshman year of college at the University of Toledo, I transferred to Kent State University. I went from being Mike Hayslip's roommate at Toledo to getting an apartment with Matt in Kent. We had the time of our lives together. I would drive home every night in the fall to coach with dad, and every night when I got back there was Matt violently yelling at the TV because he was losing to our other roommate in Madden again. Matt insisted that damn TV was always out to get him and would only act up when he was losing, it was the weirdest thing.

While Matt and I had a blast, we and had our fair share of dumb college kid moments. Looking back now, things were different when Matt was around. Matt was a leader, and the type of leader people follow out of trust. Matt and I saw the world through the same scope; I think that's why we got along. We did a lot of dumb stuff, but we took care of each other, and more importantly, he took care of my brother Dom. He treated Dom like a little brother. There was the occasional "noogie" and we messed with him, but Dom knew he had another older brother that cared about him. The summer before my junior year in college, Matt came to work for my Uncle Greg at the Garden center. Matt and I spent a lot of time together that summer, especially because the garden center was 30 minutes away from where we lived. Dom, Matt, and I would have a blast driving together. Now, Dom likes country music but Matt and I are diehard fans. The theme song for the summer was "Made in America" by Toby Keith. It's just a great song and we couldn't get enough of it. Looking back, I think it's because there isn't a better song to describe Matt. For those of you who aren't familiar, it's about a family where the mom and dad are patriotic to the max. The father is just patriotic to the core. Buys American made cars, "spends more in the store for a shirt in the back says made in the U.S.A.", and "can fix anything with WD-40 and a craftsman wrench" that was Matt.

Matt is just genuine. You get what you see, and that is something you don't find much in my generation - or at all. Like the rest of my friends, he helped me through a lot with my family. Matt had a different approach though; he knew the struggles I was having, but he would tell me "He's still your brother, and they are still your family." Sounds simple, but hearing it wasn't easy. I have a family I wouldn't trade for the world but we have been through a lot. When I told you about my brother Dom, I mentioned how protective I was. Matt knew that but he reminded me that Nick is my brother too - regardless of our relationship. As hard as that was to swallow, it's something I will never forget. Family and friends are everything. To this very day, I teach the young men my father and I coach that you won't like all your teammates, the people you work with or for, or your siblings and family at times, but at the end of the day, a team is a team. Just like in the Army I didn't like every soldier I met, but we wore the same uniform and fought the same fight. A team only succeeds when each member can put those differences to the side, stands together and move forward as one solid unit. I would tell Matt how mad I was that Nick and I fought and wouldn't speak for months, but he wouldn't hesitate to ask me for help. All I saw was Nick taking advantage of me but Matt saw something different.

I remember being in my driveway and getting a call from Nick one day after Matt and I had gotten home from work. We had worked at least ten hours in the August sun and heat and were exhausted. Nick had been dating a girl and he had gotten into a verbal fight with her. Nick had left her house and was walking through the woods somewhere, threatening to take his life. He called me frantic like the world was ending. I told Matt he doesn't need to leave my house, he was welcome to just hang out, but I had to go get my brother. I ran upstairs to get my wallet and keys and when I came down, Matt was already in my truck. He wasn't staying behind, and it just proved his point to me. You take care of your family and friends. It's one thing to make that commitment when things are going smoothly; it's another to live it when things unwrap. On our way to get Nick, I was expressing my frustration and Matt had a simple response: "you can be mad all you want, but he's your brother, and when it comes down to it, you know you'll go get him every single time. You can fight with him when we get home, but we have to get him first. I would do the same for my brother. It's just what you do for the people who rely on you. That's why he chose you to call in his time of need."

Fights happen, people argue, and sometimes things get out of control like they did between Nick and I; but at the end of the day when I lay my head down, I know my family is still my family, and until the day God calls me home I will protect them with all my heart and soul. Matt is family to me. Always has been, always will be. When things went wrong he was right there with me. Matt told me something that night when I got home that I will keep with me forever: "You know you and I are different. There is a different kind of blood that runs through our veins."

Matt and I had similar callings in life. When I joined the military I had a lot of support. He was the only one who really seemed to understand the calling I felt. He is actually the reason why I gave criminal justice a go try before I enlisted. There is no doubt that Matt could have done anything he wanted in life. He comes from a great family. He could have gone into so many fields where money and prestige were nearly guaranteed. Instead, he chose a life like I did - of honor and service. He understood when I told him the calling was inescapable. He understood when I told him it was what I was born to do. He understood when I told him I just couldn't settle for anything but what my heart told me to do.

I remember sitting on the tailgate of his truck (which is where our serious talks happened) after I made the choice to join the Army. I told him "How could I teach these kids I coach, and (God willing) my kids one day, to follow their hearts; that they can be anything they want to be; And that they have the choice to be anything or anyone they want in the world - if I wasn't going to do that myself."

I spoke with the recruiters from the Marines and Army time and time again and always found an excuse not to follow through. I remember when I took college tours with my friend Shannon; her father walked with me to look at the ROTC booth. He told me if there was anything he would redo in his life, it would be to go through with it when he wanted to join the Navy. I will never forget that. The moment you reach regret, its normally too late to change. My father's signature phrase to our team is "Opportunity is like a sunrise, if you wait too long, you'll miss it." I finally followed my heart and enlisted in the United States Army and it was the proudest moment of my life. It was no surprise to Matt when I left because he was following his calling as well. Matt began his career as a Police Officer, which I have no doubt will be filled with the honor and prestige he deserves.

Matt and I both came from families that were financially sound. We spent countless days on his parents' boat and in my family's beautiful home. Life was comfortable and without Matt's understanding of my calling, I may not have had the courage to break away from that lifestyle. I may have never left. My father has been the most supportive person in my life but he and I struggled when I told him my calling. It wasn't that he didn't support my choice - he just didn't understand it. Papi played baseball for the Navy but he was never deployed - in fact, never saw a ship. He was worried when I left because I was the first person in my family to enter the military during a time of war. I repeatedly told Matt my concerns with leaving. I made excuses like Nick and Dom needed me here, that dad wouldn't talk to me anymore, and that I wanted to finish college. He knew that none of those were true and he called me on it time and time again. I may still be sitting at home when the day comes where I tell my future kids "I almost had my dream job" and would have no adequate answer when they asked me why I never followed through.

Matt followed his heart to become a cop and that passion is what will make him incredible at it. I will never forget what Matt told me when I got hurt and the Army told me my time was done. I was crushed because I felt like the Army was taken from me. Everyone told me "You did your part; you were hurt serving our country" but they just didn't understand. I fought and clawed to stay in, but my time had come to head home. Matt told me "You trusted your heart, and you put your soul into the time you had. If the day ever came that I could no longer be a cop, as crushed as I would be, I would be at peace knowing that every day I was a cop, I was the best cop I could be, and I was living my dream." I refuse to ever reach the point of regret in my life again. I tell the young men on our football team to never take a play off, or go half speed on a sprint, because once you get in the habit of taking the easy way out, it's like quicksand; it's nearly impossible to get back out.

Like Papi said "the champ is down, but he's not out" and it's the truth. Matt was right, and I am at peace. My proudest moment is the day I left, and I thank Matt so much for that support. He convinced me to follow my heart, and it was the best choice I've ever made. As a veteran now, I have no regrets, and I can't wait until the day I get to tell my kids to follow their hearts, because it will be the most genuine lesson I will ever teach.

Mr. Minor

Before I even got to football camp as a freshman. I had something to look forward to going into high school. I went to Notre Dame Cathedral Latin (NDCL) in Chardon, Ohio and my freshman year was the first year for our new principal. His name was Mr. Waler, and he was coming over from Trinity High school in Garfield, Ohio where my cousin Matt was also going to be a freshman. My aunt and my cousins were so upset that he wouldn't be at Trinity anymore, and all I kept hearing was how amazing this guy was. Now, it's great and all that everyone seemed to really like this man. Everybody likes "cool teachers" or obviously even better a "cool principal." For me, however, I had a different reason. This wasn't just a cool principal you could joke with in the hallway. This was a new principal who didn't know my brother Nicholas. A principal who didn't know the trouble Nick had caused, which meant I had a chance to make my own name for myself. Unfortunately, as much as I love my brother Nick, his predictability is something I didn't quite have a grasp on while setting my expectations for my first year of high school. Within our first week, Nick got into a fight, and both Nick and I had the pleasure of meeting Mr. Waler together.

I dreaded another circumstance where I ended up getting labeled as "Nick Natale's brother." Mr. Waler hadn't even been principal for a full week, and before he unpacked the boxes in his office, the Natale brothers made it on his radar. I wasn't sure how to handle the looks I got from my friends when Mr. Waler would call me out and greet me by name as our group walked by. The day when I was called down to his office without Nick was the day after Nick was sent to the Carolina treatment facility. This was when the night I spend at Uncle Carl's house, and also the same night I was informed I was academically ineligible for football. I walked down to Mr. Waler's office thinking the school was going to tell me the consequences for my grades. I remember walking as slowly as possible, still processing what had happened to Nick; now this was just going to pile onto the stress. I kept thinking this is only a few weeks into my first of four years; it can only get worse from here.

Walking to his office, of course, I was lost. Being new to the school and mentally preparing for my punishment, I realized I was lost. There was a glass window where a secretary sat and answered the phone. Before I could decide if I was at the right place, Mr. Waler came to greet me. Much to my surprise, it wasn't with a stern or condescending look; it was with a concerned but welcoming smile. Instead of letting the secretary escort an already nervous and troubled kid into his office, he came to greet me himself. It sounds minor, but my father always told me to pay attention to the little things - and I did. A man running an entire high school, indeed, as new to the school as I was, he hadn't even unpacked all of his boxes when I made it into his office, yet he made it a point to come greet me himself.

As I sat down in his office, he began by asking me how I was doing. I never got in serious trouble in school, but if I had the opportunity to compile the statistics...a good 99.99% of the time I had been summoned to the principal's office in the past was punitive in nature. This was that .01%. This visit was for Mr. Waler to ask me about my brother Nick. More specifically, he asked about how I was dealing with Nick. We sat in his office and just talked. I have seen family therapists, group therapists, and had even gone with Nick countless times to speak to his therapist with him. This was different; it wasn't that those therapists didn't care, but the focus was always on helping Nick. When I was young, I was angry. Angry at Nick, angry at my family, angry at the world. I always asked myself why couldn't my family just be normal, and where was my help?

Mr. Waler didn't ask me how was my brother. He asked how *I* was. How I was dealing with Nick leaving. How *I* was dealing with school in general. He reassured me that high school was hard enough without the extra curveballs I had been thrown. Our talk was just different from anything I had experienced before. It would have been so easy for him to just tell my teachers to keep an eye on me and push me off on someone else. I wouldn't have held that against him, either; he was brand new, and I knew I wasn't the only one in school who was having issues. What made it so special was that he made the conscious choice to make a difference on a personal level. Seeing Mr. Waler in action was when I started to realize what my father meant about passion. Mr. Waler's passion for teaching and mentoring his students emanated from him. Everything he did was with that glorious smile and was for his students, faculty, and his beloved school.

Principals have so many things to deal with, but this man asked me every single morning how I was - for four years. Every single day. He would stand out front of the school and greet the students. Every morning when I walked by, there he was, and it was a different kind of look he gave me. Nick was gone and back within 18 months of Mr. Waler's initial outreach to me. Our talks weren't always about Nick; he asked me about my Mom, Dad, Dom, and life in general.

I trusted him because every single ounce of that man was genuine. I trusted him with my life, and I always will. Four years.

In the fall, Mr. Waler would ask me every day how coaching St. Rita's was going with my dad. He would ask about the kids, about dad, and about how happy he was that I found something productive to do that I enjoyed, and that kept me around the game I loved. He also knew how much spending time with my dad meant to me. I will never forget the day, my junior year in high school when my dad and I scrimmaged at NDCL on a Saturday. I remember gathering the kids around me for a pre-game speech, and as they ran out on the field, I noticed a man walking towards the field from the distance. It was him; it was Mr. Waler. I hadn't told him about the scrimmage; but, then again, it was his school. He just smiled at me. After the game, he just smiled and walked away. It took me a while to understand exactly why he did that, why he didn't come up to me after the game.

He sat and watched the entire game from a distance - just like he watched me in school. He would check in with me but he remained behind the scenes. He knew peers would pry, ask questions, start rumors. He showed me he was there to watch me and guide me. There were so many kids in that school, yet I'm convinced he knew every single kid's name, and probably their parents' names to. I'm sure he did for others what he did for me. People adored him.

I'll give you a brief history lesson on my high school Notre Dame Cathedral Latin (NDCL). Notre Dame was an all-girls school and Cathedral Latin was an all-boys school. My father actually went to Cathedral Latin his freshman year, which was the last year before it closed down. When it was re-opened years later, it re-opened as a merged Notre Dame Cathedral Latin, which is now coed. The school has a huge and beautiful campus and is run by the Sisters of Notre Dame. They were nuns who had been running the school since Notre Dame's original inception. My father was the type of dad who would tell me how school was so much different when he was young - the classic "I walked 74 miles to school each day, and both ways were uphill". He talked about how in grade school the nuns dragged him out of the class by his ear when he got in trouble or acted out. I guess you can say that over the years, the nuns have adjusted and refined their approach to more conservative, subtle tactics.

For discipline, had minors and majors. The concept was pretty self-explanatory. Minors were for minor infractions; talking, tardiness, eating in class. Once you accumulated, if I remember correctly, three minors, you received a major, which equaled detention. Like I said when I introduced you to some of my close friends, I was mighty familiar with detention. All joking aside, I acted out a lot. I'm sure a lot of it was just to get attention. I rarely got in serious trouble, but the teachers knew my name, and it sure wasn't because of my exemplary academic performance. As I mentioned before, I was an angry kid, and it caused me to pick a lot of fights in school and out. Every time my parents picked me up from detention or got a summary of all 9,567,865 minors I received that year, they would tell me they knew I was 'meant for better' but aren't parents supposed to tell you that? Well, let me tell you when the principal says that, it holds different weight.

I began to look to Mr. Waler like a hero. Each year my dad asks the kids we coach "Who's your hero?" He asks the question throughout the year. He never tells them why he does this or what the answers he's looking for are. Year after year, the answers change from Michael Jordan, Ray Lewis, Lebron James in the beginning...to answers like Mom or Dad, brothers and sisters, aunts and uncles. Real heroes are people they can always rely on, look up to, model their lives after. It wasn't until I sat down to write this book that *I* realized just how many heroes I had. Mr. Waler was every bit of a hero to me. Everyone defines a hero differently, but I am more than confident I am not the only one to call this man a hero. He took an interest in me, and made me feel like I mattered. When I would get sent to his office, he would tell me exactly what my mom and dad both told me: "You're better than this".

Sister Nancy was one of the sisters who taught at NDCL was a bit older. She taught me social studies freshman year, and I had her again junior year for history. She was such a nice lady but snappy. She was a little fire cracker, but I loved her. I used to give her a hard time, and she would write me minors like they were going out of style, but I'm

50% sure she loved me, too. Every once in a while, I would catch her trying not to laugh when I made some snippy remark in class. Even in her class, though, there were times I crossed lines. I won't say every time I got in trouble was just innocent 'boys being boys' behavior.

When I got sent to Mr. Waler's office, I expected him to slowly lose faith in me. I remember feeling guilt as I walked to his office. He had made such an effort to look out for me, and I was letting him down.' He would simply sit me down on the coach outside the office and tell me to do my homework. Sometimes he would even drop what he was doing and help me do my work. I wasn't a dumb kid; I just wasn't trying. What really changed my perspective, was when he told me I wasn't a bad kid either.

Let me tell you, I got "Best Excuse Maker" in my high school yearbook (really something to be proud of, I know). My excuses failed every single time with three people: My father, my Uncle Carl, and Mr. Waler. Every single time. The excuses that always failed began with "Well see Nick..." and Mr. Waler would cut me off. He told me to not even try. He knew I had problems with Nick, but that wasn't why I fought. As much as Nick caused tension in my house, it wasn't the only reason I acted out. He called me on my excuses like my Uncle Carl did on that Fourth of July. Mr. Waler was there for me for four years. He never quit on me. He told me something I will never forget: that all the trouble I was getting in wasn't who I was. I told him "Well, Nick and I always fight and argue and get in trouble at home" and he stopped me. He said "Well you're not home, you're here with me. You're also not Nick, your Tim, and you get to choose for yourself the type of person you want to be and the type of life you want to live...Nick doesn't get to do that for you and who knows - maybe when Nick sees you turning your life around, he will too."

To this very day, every single move I make, I do so wondering how it will affect not only Nick but both of my brothers. Mr. Waler pulled me out of a mindset that my fate was sealed and that my relationship with Nick would never change. He could have quit on me so early into school, but he didn't. He hung on and eventually so did I, and I made it through. Sometimes all you need is to know someone still believes in you no matter how many times you've failed. Just one person can change your life when you realize they still believe in you, that they haven't quit on you even if you quit on yourself. That gave me just enough strength to give everything one more shot, and here I am. Take this lesson with you. Maybe, one day, *you* will be the person to believe in someone. The one to keep them going. Be someone's hero. The day I graduated, Mr. Waler shook my hand and handed me my diploma and said "Okay Mr. Minor, you made it out." I truly don't know if I could have without him. People like him showed me the light at the end of the tunnel. I would love to meet the people who raised *him* and thank them.

That type of leadership takes passion. It takes a desire to change the world. I may have been young and naive about a lot of important things early in my life, but the one thing I never questioned was that people like Mr. Waler were the people who made the world turn. They wake up each morning making the choice to change the world. People like him make the conscious choice every day to live for others, and to make a difference, to change the world and that is exactly what he did, one person at a time.

The Blood of Calhooooon

Most of us had a neighbor growing up that we got along with and maybe even grew to be good friends with. My experience with my neighbor Chris Lanzillotti takes that to a whole new level. Chris probably spends more time at my house then I do. Somewhere along the line, he decided (or we decided) he was another son to my parents, and that is no exaggeration. We joke with Chris about how much he is over, and for coming to family dinners, but the truth is, it wouldn't be the same without Chris. He is every bit a part of our family as my brothers and I. Chris and I have been friends since about sixth grade. He found himself dealing directly with some of the tougher times my family has had. Nick and Chris had their issues directly, but Chris was different - he didn't react. Chris has a heart of gold, and time and time again, he would reach out to Nick, regardless of how poorly Nick treated him. I could never understand why Chris would call and ask if we could all hangout. No matter how bad things with Nick were, Nick was always invited.

Chris probably doesn't realize this, but he showed his true colors the last few months prior to my enlistment in the military. Since I have been in, he is still at my house, spending time with my family, and within moments of coming home on leave, Chris would be flying down the driveway. Yes, Chris drives to my house from his house 300 ft. away.

This may be the only time I admit I was nervous about going to basic training. I was in shape, and I had the motivation behind me, but it was my first time being responsible for myself. I, alone signed a contract which dictated the next four years of my life. In addition, this contract included a clause which implied I was prepared to give my life for my country, and those within that country. It was kind of a surreal feeling for me enlisting because I always wanted to be in the Army. My entire life, if you asked me my dream job, I would have told you soldier. When I left Kent State, I was "studying" criminal justice hoping it would fill my desire to serve. I was terrified of actually leaving for the military regardless of my overwhelming calling.

I had my own apartment in Kent during fall semester. I would drive to Solon every night to coach football with dad, but Tuesday and Thursday nights at about eight o'clock, Chris would come straight from school to hang out. One Tuesday night was different, because earlier that day I was approached by the recruiter on campus. I had spent a brief moment speaking with him, then went to coach without mentioning it to my dad. Chris was the first person I told that I was seriously considering the Army. Chris and I could spend 12 hours straight playing video games or watching *Always Sunny in Philadelphia*. Together we could be as immature as it gets, but Chris and I have this unspoken understanding that when it is time to be serious. This night was one of those nights. I was terrified when I told Chris because, regardless of how supportive he was, it was a big step for me. We had serious conversations before, but it was about a girl I liked or changing majors, nothing even close to this magnitude. We talked that night for hours about the pros and cons, but Chris had known me long enough to know that my mind was made up.

A month later, after I informed my family, I went to MEPS which is where you take the entrance exam (ASVAB), a physical, and officially sign your contract. The night before we stayed in a really nice hotel downtown. Just me and a bunch of young men and women who were making the same choice. This night was also the night they counted the votes for President Obama's re-election. Coming from a Republican family, I had a variety of phone calls trying to talk me out of moving forward. I couldn't sleep that night; I would be lying if I told you I wasn't fighting some serious doubts about this commitment despite my calling. I had never left home for a significant amount of time other than my year at the University of Toledo. My family is very supportive, but I had no way to verbalize the calling I had, so to them it seemed like a way for me to drop out of school, which was a reasonable reservation based on my track record of quitting when things got tough. Chris knew this was different.

I remember my phone ringing that night and expected it to be another person trying to change my mind. Honestly, if it had been, there's a chance it may have worked. It was Chris. I could hear in his voice his concern. He had been so loyal to me my entire life and helped me through some of the toughest times with Nick and my family. Chris's advice and opinions held so much weight my entire life, and this was no different. He called to ask me "are you sure this is what you want to do?" My response being yes, he told me "Well, ok. I'm with you then," which is all that I needed. His phone call was what sealed my choice to enlist. His words on that phone call could have went in either direction, and my choice may have followed. I owe Chris so much of the success I found in the military, because without him, I may not have made it there.

Chris is as loyal as they come. He has a heart of gold. I enlisted in November of 2012 and didn't ship for basic until 26 February 2013. Our Tuesday and Thursday night video games turned into nearly every night. I was nervous beyond words, but those few hours we would sit and play video games took my mind off of everything. We would laugh and laugh and before we knew it, it was the middle of the night. We would listen to the theme song from the movie Boondock Saints on repeat (The Blood of Cuchulainn). When I say repeat, I mean probably 50 times in a row, and the song is just this Irish theme music. Neither of us could ever pronounce the name, so we just called it "The Blood of Calhooooon".

The semester ended in December, so I spent the holiday season and the next two months sitting around the house. I had never had so much down time, and I spent the majority of it with Papi, taking him to appointments and just relaxing with him. The moment Chris got out of school he was at my house, and we played video games and watched *It's Always Sunny* every single night. An act of congress couldn't keep Chris and I apart those few months. I never told him how afraid I was to leave, but he knew. I never told him how nervous I was to leave my family, but he knew. The night before I left for basic training, out of nowhere, Chris looked at me and said "you know I will take care of them, right?" I knew exactly what he was referring to - my family. More specifically - my brothers. My brothers are my world, my back bone, and my biggest fear was leaving both of them because for so long the three of us kept each other going. I protected Dom, I helped Nick through his struggles, and they helped me. Chris stepped up to be their rock.

If anybody I know is a man of their word, it's Chris. If there was anybody I trusted to take care two of the most important people in my life, it was Chris. He did what he promised. He has helped my family through more than I could ever ask of anyone. Heroes to the challenge, and on top of brothers and sisters of his own, Chris took my brothers in as his own. When I left for basic I was afraid, but knowing they were in good hands made it easier. Chris and my brothers became even greater friends. Throughout my entire tour overseas, Chris was there. Most importantly the moment I came home on leave, he was there. He is the type of person you beg God to put into your life. My family adores and loves Chris. Chris isn't a guest in my family. Chris is family. To this very day he is at my house nearly every single night, talking about stocks and whatever else the world has to offer, in addition to watching "It's Always Sunny" series for the 15th time on Netflix. Our tradition and routine can't be broken. A lifetime wouldn't begin to be enough time for me to thank Chris for what he has done for my family and me. He is an incredible friend, and I couldn't imagine where I would be if I had never met Chris Lanzillotti.

The Little Irish Boy

I can honestly say the people I have met in the Army have become some of the greatest friends I have in my life. The first day of basic training we are all nervous together. You don't sleep for days, and you are constantly taking an emotional and physical beating from the Drill Sergeants. Sleep deprivation is no joke. Needless to say, you find out who your friends will be very quickly and learn to rely on them with your heart and soul immediately.

One man I met during this time who changed my life was Chris Doyle. There is absolutely no way I would be the man I am without him. He made his way into the first letters I wrote home, and from that day forward my father thought I was writing him about my bunkmate, "the little Irish boy" raised in an Irish Catholic family. I came from a family where I didn't have to worry about money, and my father had given me every opportunity, which the majority of my life I've let slip through my fingers. At 20 years old, I thought I had it all figured out until I met Chris Doyle who changed the way I see the world.

When a new soldier shows up to basic training they go to what's called "reception". It's arguably the worst part of basic training because you have no idea what to expect. You sleep for roughly six hours over four days. It's well known the Army's technique is to break you down as an individual and build you back up as a member of a team; let me just say, there are no words to explain being broken down.

I flew to basic at Fort Jackson in Columbia, SC. A "DS" (Drill Sergeant) picked us up from the airport, and we took a bus trip that seemed like an eternity. When the bus stops, so does your heart for that moment because you cannot mask the fear that comes with uncertainty. When six men in camouflage come charging at the bus with their Drill Sergeant hats pulled down over their eyes, approaching at a speed which seems humanly impossible, you cannot help but look to the man next to you and get this overwhelming feeling of gratefulness for not being alone - a feeling that he will be the one to help you through it all. Later, I would learn that man had a life that I didn't realize existed because my father had given me a life the majority of the world would give their arm for. That man next to me was Chris Doyle, and all I knew about him on the bus was that he was an African American guy from Chicago who didn't talk much. He had a look in his eye that I will never forget. I had not said a word to him other than "What is your name?" and "Where are you from?" but I knew this was the man I wanted next to me during this battle, and he was every single day for the next 10 weeks. If i was going to lay down my life for my country, I would have been proud to do it next to this man.

Chris Doyle changed my life and taught me what true friendship is. On day 1, after being yelled at until 4:00 in the morning, and our Drill Sergeants released us to find bunks for the night: "ok time to get some sleep. When you hear the alarm, it's time to get up." Little did we know, that alarm would go off after just 27 minutes.

Reception lasts about four days, on the second day, when it was meal time, I had about 3 minutes to eat. After a few bites, I had to run back to get in line, but I collapsed and I vomited the little food I had eaten. I couldn't feel my legs and as hard as I fought to get up, I couldn't. I cannot put into words the way the Drill Sergeants jumped on this opportunity to rip into me; but, it kind of feels like every adversary you ever had, every classmate you didn't get along with, and every nemesis you ever feared, gets a free pass to crush your spirit. I was in that hell when, out of nowhere, comes Chris Doyle.

I thought it was bad when they were laying into me for being "weak," but I couldn't believe how they threatened Chris to leave me down and carry on without me. They screamed: "Leave him! He's just going to slow you down. He's weak!!!" Chris refused. A man I barely knew saw me down and refused to leave without me, regardless of it's personal costs to him. To this day, I don't know what was wrong with me. I don't know whether I got sick from the food or what it was, but I felt paralyzed. So, paralyzed and out of it, in fact, that while getting pushed to the ground and yelled at by what seemed like an entire army of Drill Sergeants, I have no idea how Chris managed to clean up my mess and throw me over his shoulder and run what seemed like miles to catch up with the rest of our group. Chris set me down like nothing had happened and this was just another day for him. That night we had about 45 minutes to shower and get ready for bed, which was all the time they gave us to get to know the men with whom we were about to spend the next ten weeks with. Making your way to the Drill Sergeants bad side the first couple days is every new soldier's nightmare, but fortunately for us, day four comes around and it's time to get back on the bus and leave reception. I thought the first bus ride seemed like an eternity; this one seemed even longer as we contemplated what hell on earth awaited us next. When we finally arrived, the bus stopped and instead of six Drill Sergeants ascending upon us, there were waves of them running at us which they refer to as the "shark attack". After about two hours of being called every name imaginable and doing more physical exercise than I thought possible, it was time for us to break into groups (platoons) within our company. All of a sudden, here comes Chris Doyle getting "lit up" once again by the Drill Sergeants because he refused to enter our bay until everyone else made it in first. At this point I am in awe of this man, who absolutely didn't care about repercussions to himself - because the DS made it clear that the last man in the bay "was in for a world of hurt." Chris would rather it be him than watch one of these people he barely knows experience that pain.

Just like before, Chris is outside getting "smoked" (a term in the military used to described vigorous amounts of physical corrective training) and somehow, I had this rush come over me that it was my turn to sacrifice myself to help him. I didn't realize it until weeks later that his instinctual acts of teamwork, compassion, and leadership rubbed off on me and inspired me to help a friend in need. I wasn't even two steps out the door when I get shoved to the ground by a drill sergeant. I felt invincible and I sprung right back up. I felt like there was not a single thing in this world that could stop me from standing by Chris's side until it's over. It felt like hours on the concrete doing pushups, sit-ups, and whatever else you can imagine while having an army of drill sergeants call us every name in the book through bull horns. When it was finally over, it took every ounce of energy we had left to even make it up on one knee, only to walk inside and see our bags dumped open, clothes ripped up, pictures of our families scattered across the floor. None of it mattered, though because even the drill sergeants knew they had built a bond that they couldn't break.

After a day of what seemed like hell on earth, it was finally time to learn how to make our beds (when you go to basic you learn how to make your bed all over again and its inspected every morning at 0400) and find our bunkmates. It's not like high school where you get to pick your partner. The Drill Sergeants pick you a bunkmate. I noticed they seemed to make pairs of "polar opposites." You guessed it, "Natale, Doyle, fourth bunk on the right."

That night, Chris and I didn't sleep at all, I had to know what made a man like Chris tick, and I needed to ask him why he came back for me. Chris told me he had spent his teenage years in a gang - deep in a gang doing things he spent nights praying he could take back. I knew nothing about gangs except what the media reported. I could see in his eyes the regret and determination he had to change his life.

Chris proceeded to tell me he joined the Army Reserve, which meant he would be going back to Chicago after training. He enlisted so he could get out of the life he previously led. I had to ask: "Well, why didn't you just go active duty so you never had to go back?" To this day, I remember his response exactly: "If I never go back, how am I going to get my mom and family out? I can't leave them behind because they need me, and I would rather die than leave them behind." My heart dropped because before me sat a man who refused to leave his family behind and would rather lose his life than just start a new life without them.

I came from a life Chris would drool over, and up until this moment, I had taken advantage of everything I had. Chris told me he used to wake up and pray he would make it to school without taking a stray bullet. I was ashamed that biggest concern before school was if I had to show up in Mom's van or Dad's Porsche.

Chris and I made a pact. We were going to change the world. We were going to be the best soldiers we could be, and we both promised that whether family, friends, or people we barely knew, we were never going to leave anyone behind. Chris' motto was "all or none," which meant we all come out together or none of us. I didn't sleep that night, but that next day felt like I was reborn. Chris and I took basic training in stride, and we fought every single obstacle they threw at us like there was no tomorrow. More importantly, for the first time in my life, I realized what I was truly capable of. I realized this because I loved the feeling of knowing people were relying on me to lead them, especially Chris. We were unstoppable together and our entire company knew it.

It wasn't just our exemplary performance that separated us. We fed off each other's passion, motivation, and desire. I was named team leader, squad leader, and then PG, which meant I was in charge of the entire platoon. Those accomplishments are to this day some of my proudest moments. Chris was right there every step of the way.

My drill sergeant told me that, as a leader, you eat last to make sure all of your soldiers get food, and if there are any scraps, then you eat. As a leader, you are the last person to reap the benefits of your team's success and the first one to accept its consequences. Chris never had to, but he was always the second last to eat and would wait until I sat down to make sure we both had an even amount. I cannot remember one time Chris put himself before someone else.

Chris pulled me out of some very tough situations. He never held it over my head. He lived by a code that you can't teach. The last memory I will share with you happened the last two days of basic training. Family day and graduation are the two days where your family comes to watch graduation ceremonies and spend some time with their new soldiers. Family day arrived, and our families sat in bleachers looking across the parade field at the edge of the woods. They didn't know, but we were in the woods waiting to charge out with smoke, simulation grenades, and gunfire going off! We stormed the field. Chills ran through my body because all I could think about was looking cool and making my family proud. Chris was right next to me and just when the grenades start going off he looks at me and says "Remember buddy, all or none".

Those ten weeks that Chris and I spent together seemed like a lifetime. He changed my life. I could sit here and tell you stories forever about Chris because every day was another day he made an impact on someone's life - on my life. My father told me for as long as I can remember "you can count your true friends on one hand," Man was he right. Chris met my family, and I met his mother and sister that day. Right before Family Day was over, we were looking at gear when my dad saw Chris put a pair of new books back on the shelf. Everyone who saw Chris put those boots back knew it was because of the cost. We had spent ten weeks in the same pair of boots with our heels bleeding, and your feet swollen. These new Rocky boots were like pillows on your feet. My dad walked right up to Chris and said "You pick out the boots you want. You are my sons brother, which makes you my son. You my friend make God smile." Chris was not only my new brother, he was welcomed into my family like I knew he would be.

Chris and I stayed very close for the next two years while I completed my tour overseas. He never hesitated to tell me how proud of me he was, and I couldn't tell you how many times he had the chance to join me on active duty. Time and again, Chris declined. There was just no way he would leave his family behind, "all or none". He was working three jobs. When I was coming home from Germany, and we were trying to find a time to meet while I was on leave. On 14 August 2015, we were talking about how two and a half years later, he still wore those boots my dad bought him because he said "these boots are a gift from a man I will never forget. He is the type of man who I would lay my life down for." No amount of training, toughness, or preparation can prepare you for what happened next.

On 16 August 2015, Chris Doyle was gunned down in the streets of Chicago. At the age of 21, God had called him home. I couldn't believe it, I genuinely thought my heart had stopped. I had been alive 23 years, and I can say from the bottom of my heart that I had never felt pain like this before.

People do not realize the types of relationships you build in the military. The bonds just aren't the same as in the civilian world. You don't make friends in the military, you make family. That day my brother was called home. Chris told me he would rather die than leave his family behind, and he took that promise to his grave. I hadn't seen Chris in over two years, and the moment I found out he was killed it felt like he had been killed right infant of me. I fell on my knees in my kitchen, Kelsey Rose was upstairs in my room under the impression I just went to check my phone downstairs, soon she saw me in a mood she hadn't seen in the four years we had been together. My whole life I had been the tough one of my brothers, the leader in the military, the one everyone else came to with their pain, but I couldn't help but drop my head into her lap and cry like the world had ended. Chris wasn't just another one of my friends, he was the one who promised me we would change the world together. He changed my life in a way that I will probably never be able to fully describe. He changed the way I see the world. He changed the way I live, he changed the type of man I am. All I could think about is that the world is full of corrupt and evil people, and the most genuine and selfless person I know was gone.

Chris was like my father, he lived by the code that he preached to others. He stuck by his family and those who relied on him when he had every opportunity and reason to leave. It's not always about having something to lose that makes some choices in life worth it. But it's about having something to choose. He gave up a life he knew would be in his own best interest and chose to live a life that would pro-tect his family at home. He made a choice to stick by them at whatever cost. He completely changed the course of his life. He knew there was a very real danger for himself if he returned home to Chicago and the life he had known before the Army, but he drove forward. He is the reason I will never quit on those who rely on me. He is the reason why I will always offer myself up for others. he is the reason I am here today to share this all with you. Chris is gone, but he's not forgotten. The only way he would truly be gone is for me to not fulfill his legacy by sharing with the world the type of man he was. He is still the backbone to how I live my life.

Invest your heart and soul into whatever it is you do to-day because tomorrow is never promised. Every morning, God gives me the opportunity to wake up again and fulfill Chris's legacy. Chris may not have lost his life on the battle-field, but there is no doubt in my mind that Chris gave his life for the ones he loved. I pray this chapter gives Chris's family some peace even though it only begins to describe what Chris has done for me. Chris's mother was so kind to allow me to get Chris the most beautiful headstone. I would have built Chris a monument if I could. God gave me the chance to go visit Chris on the third of July 2016. It was so peaceful to just sit there and be with him. I just sat there and talked to him, and I left my Army name tape and my SGT rank on his grave because all the success I had in the Army I attribute to Chris. He could have left me down that first day but he didn't, and I owe him the world for that.

I made Chris a promise that I will keep. One person at a time, I will change the world. I will not only live his legacy, but I will build it. Lead the way Chris. I know you have a better vantage point on me now. Shine your light, and we will light up the world buddy. I miss you buddy. I live my life for you, brother.

The Little Engine That Could

I never would have thought in a million years I would fear someone smaller than me. I was always the smallest of my friends, so if I ran into someone smaller than me, there was a good chance I could win that battle.

This was not the case when I met Drill Sergeant Brito during the shark attack of basic training. This man stood roughly 5 foot six inches, but his low center of gravity did not hinder the power of his Spartan kick. I mentioned when talking about Chris Doyle, getting thrown to the ground when coming to Chris's aid outside of our bay. Well, the boot I took to the chest sending me to the ground belonged to DS Brito. This man was the definition of what you would assume a DS would be. He instilled the fear of God into each of us that day in a way I did not realize was humanly possible. But he is also a huge reason Chris Doyle and I became the team we were. This man spent the next ten weeks hovering over me like I can't explain. He played a critical role in who I am today.

Chris Doyle brought his toughness from the streets with him tenfold. When Chris and I came back inside the bay that day to collect all of our scattered gear. DS Brito found his way right next to us just inches from our face. How Chris believed now would be a good time to whisper in my ear "man this guy is like the little engine that could" without realizing DS Brito's low center of gravity gave him the ability to hear this wonderful comment. This was all he needed to hear to solidify our positions at the top of his "shit list".

I can't tell you how he did it, but DS Brito made his way into every aspect of my life. From that first day, it became impossible for me to escape this man's grasp. Years later, I still wake up in the night hearing his voice in my ear. The moment I woke up in the morning he was across the bay piercing my soul with a gaze stemming from a dark abyss under his Drill Sergeant hat. It took me a few weeks to figure out why, but he took a liking to making my life specifically difficult. You may think I'm joking, but he was everywhere. It may have been the sleep deprivation, but I began to juggle the idea that there may have been clones of him because of the borderline overwhelming nature of his presence.

My entire life up until this point, I was completely content with living in the shadows. My father always told me he knew I was capable of much more, but aren't all parents "supposed" to tell you that? DS Brito forced me out of my shell. He forced me to realize my potential, but most of all, he forced me to realize what it meant to lead. Everything he taught me about leadership was exactly how I felt about my life prior to the military with my little brother Dominic. He taught me to thrive in those moments when everyone looks at you with that look in their eyes like a deer in headlights. My entire life, I fell short of my potential, but there is something about that feeling when I know that everyone is relying on me that forces me to put my heart into it. He forced that out of my soul.

Most men grow up with naturally born strengths and weaknesses. DS Britos strength was searing teamwork, loyalty, and fear into your soul. He made you realize very quickly that life was a lot easier as a group, and I wanted nothing more than to be out front. Chris had given me the fire to crush any obstacle basic training had to throw in front of me. I had the best PT score and was at the top of performers for every single training event; but, still, this man was down my neck regardless of my performance. He didn't care about who was on top. In fact, he was never in front; he was in the back of a run or march. No matter how much I tried to impress him, he just yelled more and more. Nothing I did was enough for him until the day came when I was put in charge of the platoon. He told me it didn't matter how fast you lead, if your team isn't willing to follow. He kept telling me "they will follow your every footstep, but its up to you where those footsteps lead."

Most of us have found at some point in our lives we take a split moment off from giving something our all. Sometimes its "fatigue" or maybe you just assume nobody is looking, but that wasn't an option when I had forty soldiers looking to me for strength in their moments of weakness. This was impossible for me for 10 weeks. Something about when you've done enough pushups that your arms feel like one thousand pounds, gives you an overwhelming urge to take even the slightest break when DS Brito turns around. However, it becomes extremely difficult to do so when said DS is two inches from your face counting the reps with his bullhorn looking right at you with a gaze that could give

Superman chills. I hated it, but it made me....me. He refused to let me sell myself short even for a single moment. He told me time and time again that the moment I quit, or even throttled down, was when my team would tumble.

My dad used to tell me "trust me, there is a method to my madness." There was definitely a method to my father's madness. In fact, his madness is what led me to seek my path in the military. DS Brito *definitely* had the madness part covered, but it took me until the last week to realize the method portion co-existed as well. His passion to lead and train soldiers is unprecedented. His desire to make us all the best was something I will never forget. I will take it with me in everything I do.

I will never forget one of our last days in basic, and I promise you, every single time it rains I remember that day like it was yesterday. I was our "PG" which was the highest leadership position for our platoon. We were cleaning our weapons to turn in, and at the time you don't know, but it is impossible to have your weapon "inspection ready". You could clean it for hours, have the entire platoon check it, but every time you bring it up to him, you fail. With each failure, I had to do 20 pushups. Not just my failures, everybody in my platoon who failed would go back to cleaning, and I would do 20 pushups. I remember about 100 Pushups in, I look up, fatigued, to see Chris Doyle in the back corner standing up, dusting his hands off. Chris had been doing pushups each time I had to just so I knew I wasn't alone. Seeing something like that gives me a fuel that I will never be able to fully describe. He didn't do it for attention, he did it for me. Countless times he had offered himself up for me and our team. Sacrifice is the center support beam in a team dynamic, and he reminded me it daily. Now it was my turn. I didn't resent my platoon for failing, I wanted them to know I was willing to do whatever it took for them to believe in their hearts I wouldn't quit on them.

We were cleaning weapons under the pavilion in the middle of our company area, but the pushups had to be outside where it was pouring rain. I couldn't get up fast enough, every time I finished a set, someone else failed but I wouldn't quit. I refused to let my soldiers see me quit. Out of nowhere Chris comes out to push right next to me in the pouring rain. I couldn't make the next part up if I wanted to. I must have done over 400 pushups. I could barely stand up, but my entire platoon had stacked their weapons and come to push beside me. Some of my soldiers were literally holding onto my shirt pulling me up as I lay face down into the pavement just to help me keep pushing. In my head, all I kept hearing was DS Brito telling me if I quit they would quit. I had to keep going. DS Brito came storming over yelling "Natalie it looks like you've gained their respect. All of you push until I get tired!" but I will never forget as he turned to walk away I caught him smiling. It was what he wanted the whole time: to see me sacrifice myself for them, and them for me.

My life will never be the same after meeting DS Brito. He is my hero. Not only did he show me what it meant to lead, but he showed me that regardless how tired and beaten you feel, as leader you must put your heart and soul into everything you do. I don't mean half the time or when it matters, but every second of every day, and they will follow. The team I had in basic are still some of the best friends I have today. The way you trust people in the military is different. I can't explain it. I know that if I haven't spoken to someone in years, if the day comes when it's time to fight, we are all in it together until God calls us home. My life will never be the same after he showed me that, not even as a civilian. Good things happen to good people, but truly great things happen to those who are willing to continuously offer themselves up in sacrifice for the betterment of those around them - for those who rely on them.

DS Brito called me "Luigi" (because I was Italian) or "Natalie" (like a woman's name) the entire time, regardless how many times I tried to tell him the correct pronunciation. However, I should have caught on that it is simply impossible to "correct" a Drill Sergeant. The day he met my father, he looked right at me and smiled while he said "Mr. Natale, (proper pronunciation) so great to meet you." I couldn't help but smirk, but as weird as it may sound, I interpreted that as earning his respect, which meant the world to me. That night, he told me all I needed to hear to pull myself out of any dark time the military, or my life in general would throw my way. He said "Natale, you are a remarkable soldier, and I would follow you anywhere, any day." A man that I honestly could never repay for what he has done for me, my hero, had just given me the motivation to unlock everything within my heart to ensure he never regretted those words. My platoon photo is framed in my room, regardless of the fact DS Brito refused to join us. He stood directly behind the camera man, where his eyes once again receded into the dark abyss under that hat. For any young man or woman reading this, if you ever answer the call I did to join the United States Army and attend basic training, regardless of how helpful you think you are be-ing...never touch a DS hat. Trust me.

He's Like a Piece of Iron

One of my all-time favorite movie quotes is from Rocky when Ivan Drago says "He's like a piece of Iron." For those of you who have failed at living life and have never seen the fourth Rocky movie, the quote in itself encompasses the whole concept of Rocky Balboa. He isn't the best fighter, and he found himself the underdog multiple times, but there wasn't a bone in his body that knew what it meant to quit. Each time this big Russian knocked him down, Rocky got right back up.

When I was in basic training, I met a soldier who had that heart like Rocky, and as corny as it sounds, it's the truth. You can't teach heart like this, and honestly, most people in our world will look right past people like him without even realizing how incredible they are. You can't beat someone who refuses to quit, and even when you think you have, that person is still there fighting for everything you are taking advantage of to make their dreams reality.

We encounter people in our everyday lives who just have God given talent, and I've even found myself looking at these people with jealousy and anger because everything just seems so simple for them. Whether its sports, or book smarts, anything, there is always someone out there who is "naturally" better. When I got to basic training, I met some great people and a very wide variety of people. I had a fire in my stomach because I knew this could not end up being another instance where I sold myself and my family short. There were a few instances where I found myself being the "naturally gifted" solider, and for once, I refused to let that go to waste. I've seen people everywhere who had God given opportunity to excel but wasted it, and that wasn't going to be me anymore.

One of my strongest abilities in basic training was combatives, and I have my brother Nicholas to thank for that. Growing up with Nick was like having your own personal underground cage fighting ring in the house free of charge.

I remember letting my early success get to my head, and one particular Saturday morning I got a little bit of a wakeup call. It wasn't the wakeup call you would expect, but I can promise you it's one I will never forget. We did Army combatives normally every Saturday morning, but when you have a group of let's say 30 males sleeping in a bay who think they are the next G.I. Joe, they tend to make their own schedule when the doors close for the night. For some reason, we came to the conclusion that as long as we made a circle around the two-people fighting on the marble floor and cleaned up the scuff marks, that meant it was somehow safe and the Drill Sergeants would never know. Now looking back on it, if you asked me if I would do it again, I would say absolutely yes, because as dumb as it may be, it was a bonding experience I'll never forget. If you lost, that meant you had to make someone's bed for them the next morning, or do their laundry; very high stake stuff. I would be lying if I said I was fortunate enough to be winning a decent amount, but I was challenged one night by the least likely competitor, Jordan Elmore. Honestly, until this night, I will admit I didn't have respect for Elmore like I did for some of my closer friends because he was reserved and kept to himself. I assumed he wasn't as "naturally gifted" as me when it came to fighting (shout out once again to my brother Nick). Let me tell you right now, I fought some men who could probably bench press a train, and others who were built the size of a train and won, so I was pretty confident it would be a quick victory.

Jordan was like Rocky Balboa. I honestly felt like I was fighting a "piece of iron." I was throwing everything I could imagine at him, and even if it knocked him straight to the ground, he was up before I could even catch my breath. My arms felt like jello , and I had to ask myself, how do I beat someone if he refuses to quit? How do you beat someone who wants something more than you, because no matter how great I thought I was, Jordan got up every single time he was knocked down and charged me like it was the only thing keeping him alive. Let me tell you something, as great as being "naturally talented or gifted" may be, I would take what Jordan has every single day if I could. It's irreplaceable, and when it comes down to it, my whole life I knew I wasn't the best at everything, but if I only had half the heart, passion and determination Jordan had to succeed and even to be part of a team, the opportunities are endless. Heart, however, isn't God given. It can be found, deep within yourself, if you look hard enough.

Jordan and I went round after round, until that ring of soldiers around us called the fight a draw because it had gone for so long. This was the first time this had happened since our inception. I remember standing there leaning on my bed, praying I wouldn't collapse out of exhaustion, when Jordan came over, patted me on the shoulder, and went right back to his bunk to continue the letter he was writing to his family prior to our brawl. That night I remember looking at Jordan wondering what made him so confident that he wouldn't lose. What made him so sure it wouldn't be a ten second fight? Maybe he wasn't sure, maybe he was just willing to accept the risk of failure, knowing that if he did fall short, he had given every single ounce of energy imaginable at the attempt. I don't think Jordan hit me once, but he fought like it was his last day. Regardless how many times he was knocked down, it wasn't over until it was over and if he was going down, he was going down swinging. Jordan Elmore showed me heart, and this wouldn't be the last time he showed me just what true heart actually meant. Someone like Jordan is who you want right next to you when it's time to go fight, right by your side when things seem unbearable, because people like Jordan don't quit.

People like Jordan stick with you until the end. People like Jordan give you everything they have in their heart and soul. People like Jordan don't fight for themselves, they fight to show everyone they are in it until the end. He wouldn't quit on us. We could trust that he would give us his entire heart and soul in everything we did.

I honestly wish I knew the words to explain how relationships in the military are just different than anything I had experienced in the civilian world. It took me a long time to realize why I trusted these men and women so quickly, and then it hit me. Yes, the day may come when we go to combat and our lives are entrusted in each other's hands. But we weren't in combat - we were in training. I trusted them because I saw how someone like Jordan was willing to give me his heart and soul, just to assure me if the day came when we did go fight, we were both in it until it was over. It's honestly is an indescribable feeling. I would be lying if I said everyone in the military was the best of friends. Not everyone gets along, but its unspoken that if the day comes, we are all in it together until the day God calls us home. Army, Navy, Air Force, Marines, Coast Guard, jokes are jokes, but united we stand. I teach the players my father and I coach that very mindset. To succeed in anything you do in life, you need to do it with passion and for those around you. Success is great, but the feeling you get when you watch someone else succeed and know you helped them get there is unprecedented.

One of my most memorable experiences was when we did our night infiltration course. We all had our gear on, hadn't slept, and were in this trench, which must have been ten feet tall. At what felt like 2 in the morning, we must have been waiting in the trench for hours. We can't see over the top, and it's not until a DS comes over the loud-speaker instructing us to climb up the wall and out of the trench that we had any idea what was in store for us. You can't see anything. All we knew was if you saw a flare shoot up into the air, you were to freeze. This was a simulation like we were approaching a beach. You were instructed to "skull drag" which means exactly what it sounds like. Dig your face in the sand, hold your rifle, and army crawl.

You have no idea how long the course is. All you know is there is razor wire two feet above you, so you can't stand up. Machine guns are firing over your heads, and you see the tracer rounds, and before I know it, BOOM! A simulation grenade went off two feet from my ear. Anyone who has army crawled before knows it gets tiring. Slap some body armor on, add a helmet and put a rifle in one hand and the fact you're not crawling on carpet or grass, but sand for what seems like miles, and that becomes the icing on the cake. I remember when one of the flares went off I was laying there thanking God he gave me two seconds of rest. I can't pick my head up so I look to my left, the flare drops, and there's Jordan right next to me, dragging away.

I can't describe the feeling I got when he said these simple words "Come on man, its gotta end sometime." He was right. Obviously, the course would have to end at some point, and just the little reminder that I wasn't out there alone was all I needed. To see Jordan once more, with his impenetrable spirit, lit a fire. Fire or not, my arms felt like jello, a feeling you experience frequently in basic. Maybe that's why the DS keeps going when he knows you're tired, because he wants you to realize what I just realized...maybe there is a method to their madness. Sometimes it takes seeing the fatigue beating up on a teammate to give you strength you never knew you had; that last little bit of fight left in your soul to keep you going just long enough.

I wish I could make this next part up, but right when I found myself begging it was almost over, someone grabs my foot. I roll to my side and there is Chris Doyle, holding my right foot. For that moment, I thought back to Dom growing up. I knew Chris needed me more than I needed that moment of rest. As I lay there digging deep down in my soul for the strength to drag him when out of nowhere someone grabbed my armor and pulled me out. We had reached the end. Jordan had grabbed me by the vest and pulled me out from under the wire and Chris came right out after me holding my foot.

Moments like these I will tell my kids about, but not in the context of "guess what kind of cool stuff dad did" but to reiterate my point that you need people to help you through some of the toughest moments in life. You will find yourself in both roles throughout your life. The one who people look to in their time of need, and the one in need. It's really up to you how you act in those moments. Jordan really changed my life. My father had preached heart and teamwork my whole life, and I always heard it, but it was an amazing experience to see someone like Jordan living it. I honestly don't think I have ever told anyone these two stories before. I can't thank Jordan enough for what he showed me. My father told me time and time again I could do anything I wanted when I grew up if I was willing to put my heart and soul into it and trust those around me. Jordan is a living testament to that.

Double Threat

The day I received my orders to report to Germany might have been one of the most nerve wracking days of my life. I think I was more nervous that day than when I left for basic training. The first couple of days in country, I completed administrative paperwork and basic classes to get acclimated to my new duty station where I would be spending the next two years of my life. I lived in old Nazi barracks, which everyone referred to as the "crack house" and I soon figured out why. The barracks were falling apart and were so old there was mold almost everywhere you looked. But, it could always be worse.

I will never forget the first friend I made in Germany. His name was SGT Kamien Stanford (Stan). A few days later, I began PT at 0630 in the morning and workout with my new company. One of our senior leaders is demonstrating how to do this crazy sit-up where your partner holds your feet and you execute a sit-up but you actually need to stand up at the end of it. He calls up "SGT Stan" who is an African American soldier who stands maybe 6'0 and 200LBS of solid muscle. SGT Stan gets up and walks to the middle and points at me, and calls me to be his partner. I'm asking myself what on God's earth made this mammoth of a man call me to be his partner. He didn't even know my name yet.

After PT that day, he asked me if I wanted to go to the DFAC, which was our dining facility, and we just sat there and talked. He told me about being in country, what to expect, what to train for, and most importantly what not to do. Most of what I just mentioned was what you can expect from most leaders, but Stan was a different bread entirely. He was top tier in every aspect of life. In the military, you have a chain of command, and most of your leaders at the lower levels work with you on a more personal level. Stan was not in my chain of command. We were just in the same company. We didn't even work together. But he went out of his way to mentor me, to make me feel welcome, and to ease my nerves just because he had been in my shoes.

He grew to be like an older brother to me. He was a different type of friend. He was the friend to come call me out in the gym when he saw I was just cheating myself, he would correct me during the day if he saw me goofing off. But the best part - he would come find me during lunch breaks and teach me his job. He told me it was going to make me a "double threat".

A lot of people in life teach you because it's their job or responsibility, but very few teach you simply because they want to see you succeed. Stan told me something I've only heard once in my life: "I'm going to make you better than me" which to me seemed humanly impossible. How often in your life are you willing to spend your time to make someone better at something than you are? People in today's world want to be the best individuals they can be. People wonder why they don't find success when they work so hard to make themselves better. Don't get me wrong, there is nothing wrong with challenging yourself every day to be the best you can be. But true success comes when you challenge those around you to work even harder and to succeed with you; when you offer yourself up to see them succeed.

I tell my football team it may feel great to score a touchdown, but it's an even better feeling when you throw a block that gets your friend into the end zone. Stan did that for me, time and time again. Stan was the guy everybody went to for EVERYTHING. I am not exaggerating. He could answer every question you had, and there was no task he couldn't complete. If, for some reason, Stan didn't know, he would find out, and that's what made him "mission essential". There was no mission that Stan wasn't a part of, and I had made up my mind. That was going to be me, and Stan was determined to help me get there.

The day finally came when we were deploying to a European country for a NATO training exercise, and my name got called. The feeling that was coursing through my veins is indescribable. It was only a training exercise, but to me, it was my opportunity. Take a wild guess at who was in the Task Force with me: Stan. He was communications and I was operations. Together, we were tasked to set up and operate the tactical operations center so we could talk and communicate with our Aircraft (A/C) and our foreign allies to successfully operate. We spent the next few weeks packing gear and attending brief after brief. The day finally came when it was time to leave. I left a few days early to go to another country about half the distance as a checkpoint for the A/C flying and this was definitely my chance to prove myself. I was tasked with communications as well because I only had three other people with me: our LT, my platoon sergeant, and another soldier to help me.

The time finally came to prove I was a "double threat", and it worked flawlessly. Stan and his training paid off. I was following in his footsteps. While in Germany I had a phone to communicate with in family, but in this country I didn't. I called my grandpa every day for the last couple years, and it was tough for me to imagine what was going on at home without me calling him. He just didn't understand why I had to go on this mission, and the night before I left, I was informed Nick had taken another attempt on his life. I knew I had to focus on the mission, but one night I found myself sitting up on my cot just looking out of the tent into the rain. Stan's cot was right across from mine. He came and sat next to me and said one of the simplest things possible. "It gets easier, man."

He sat there and listened to me talk to him for hours. We both had a 16-hour shift coming, but he didn't care. He just listened. He didn't feel pity for me. He showed compassion and understanding, and there is a critical difference in that. He taught me to challenge myself and push forward when faced with difficulty. More importantly, he showed me he would never quit on me and he would be there to lift me up when I fell. He taught me to embrace what my father told me about not spending my life being average. Stan taught me what it meant to have people rely on you. He taught me to be the soldier I am today. That night when we finished talking it was the middle of the night, but he told me to get dressed in workout gear and follow him.

This man and his physical abilities were unprecedented in my 21 years on earth. I did as he requested. We had arrived at his destination and let me tell you it is not what you want to see at 3 in the morning. We went to an "obstacle course" which the local military had created for workout purposes. It was a sanctuary to soldiers like Stan and I. We were climbing ropes, cargo nets, and trees and it was tough but incredible. Stan made it look easy, and I realized why he brought me there. Why he picked me that first day to be his partner in the sit-up demonstration. He saw something in me, and he told me that that night. He told me he saw himself as a younger soldier when he saw me. Most of all, he told me he saw the future of the Army in me, and that meant the world to hear from a man like him. To hear that from a man who was a top tier soldier like Stan, was a dream come true.

He didn't slow down on the obstacle course, he didn't let up. He made me chase him, even though he knew it would take time. He made me work to be the best I could be, to be better than he was. Stan made me want to be great, he made me put in the work, he held me accountable, he made me invest my heart and soul into what he taught me, and I followed his every footstep.

He knew I was having a rough night, but he didn't just feel pity and let me moan and groan. He taught me to use it as fuel and motivation. He told me that he knew my grandpa missed me, but asked me if I could imagine the happiness in his face if I brought home an award, and that is exactly what I did. I received my first award on that operation and I attribute it to the tools which Stan had provided me.

My father had told me from such an early age that life is so much easier when you show people they have a reason to believe in you. "Show the world how excellent you are, and that they cannot live without you," my father would say. Stan was telling me the same thing and he had never met my father. How could this be? How could two people who have never met be saying the same thing? I trusted them both with my life, so I invested in what they were telling me. I made myself needed, and I made myself irreplaceable to that unit. I wholeheartedly offered myself in sacrifice to see my team succeed. I would be there when Stan needed me, and most of all, I would be there when my unit needed me. I promised Stan I would make him proud that night, and he gave me the rank off his chest. He was a Sergeant (E5/ SGT), and that was my dream. I knew I could be a leader, but I wanted those stripes and everything they stood for. I wore that rank under my collar for the remainder of the two years overseas. Something that seemed so simple meant the world to me. Sometimes, that all it takes is for one person to believe in you with their heart and soul. That rank is in my room this very day right next to my bed, and even as a civilian, it inspires me every single day I wake up to live the way Stan wanted me to live.

Stan was making me into someone he could trust to lead when he was gone. Unfortunately, that came sooner than I could have ever imagined. Stan and I had done some drinking the Friday before Mother's Day, and I spent all day the next day sleeping off a hangover. I didn't go out with him Saturday night. On the way home Sunday morning, Stan was killed in a brutal car accident on the Autobahn on Mother's Day of 2014. There were three other friends of ours who were in the car with him. Fortunately, they all survived but they were significantly injured.

I didn't find out what had happened until Monday morning when we all showed up for normal PT formation at 0630. We were all formed up like normal but there was something off. Something was wrong. When our Battalion Commander and Command Sergeant Major, came out we knew something had to be going on. They brought us all around them in a "horseshoe" and told us Stan was killed and one of the soldiers who was in our company and in the car, was in the hospital. 50 grown men and women who were as tough as they come fell to their knees. You can pre-pare for war all day, every day, but you never expect to lose a fellow soldier in a way like this. My heart sank, he wasn't just a friend; to me he was my hero. He taught me nearly everything I knew about being a soldier. He was gone just like that, and I was supposed to be there. No matter how many people try to tell me not to, I will wonder forever if there is something I could have done. I had just been with him less than 48 hours before, and I wasn't there when he died because of a hangover.

I felt guilt and pain that took months to even become bearable. My father told me something, which I can't thank him enough for. I had explained to my father the impor-tance of Stan in my life and how afraid I was to be without him, and to train without him. I had spent the first nine months of my tour chasing him to be the best soldier I could be, and all of a sudden, he was gone. My father told me "pick yourself up, dust yourself off, Stan trained you for a reason. What would Stan say to you if he saw you moping like this?"

It was blunt but it was the truth. Stan wasn't gone; he was just looking over me from a better vantage point. I needed to make him proud and not let what he had done for me go to waste. Stan's favorite quote was from Muhammad Ali: "I'll show you how great I am!" and it fit Stan perfectly. That is exactly what I intended to do. It was time for me to show Stan just how great I was, because without him I may have spent my military career "falling into the shadows" as he used to say, instead of showing everyone that they need Tim Natale.

Anyone who has attended a military memorial service is familiar with roll call. They call the soldier's name three times. "SSG Stanford." No response. "SSG Kamien Stanford." Silence. SSG Kamien A. Stanford." The room is silent. Your heart sinks knowing that he is not there anymore. I was fighting with every ounce I had to hold back the tears. I was outside the window ready to fire my rifle as part of the twenty-one-gun salute. On que, we take aim, "fire!" And I can't lift up my arm. I do not know why; it was just numb from standing with it behind my back for so long. I could barely hold the rifle but I fired my three rounds on que. As embarrassed as I was after, my friend approached and said "you know that was Stan, right?" My look of confusion must have been a subtle request for more information. He said "You know Stan hated being normal. He did that to your arm to make sure his salute was just the right amount of different." I laughed, but maybe he was right. Stan sure did hate following a group; he always led from the front. I still believe to this day that numbness was Stan's unorthodox reminder to me that I was meant to stand out of the crowd.

He refused to let me fall into a crowd and blend in. To this day, I wake up every morning knowing where ever he is, he is believing in me, and that is the fuel I needed to stand out, to excel, to never accept defeat, and to pour my heart and soul into everything I did and everyone around me. I will never cheat myself or those who rely on me. I will strive until the day God calls me home to be as great of a man as Stan was. Thank you, Stan. I hope heaven has the gym you imagined it would have. I love you buddy. With your strength, I will lead the way.

Somebody Call Somebody!

If you were to ask me after my first encounter with Jalen Kendricks, if I thought we would end up becoming as close as brothers, I would have laughed. I ran into him for the first time in AIT at Fort Rucker, Alabama, which is where I did my job training after boot camp. He was the obnoxious soldier who kept advertising his hair cutting business called "Kendrix Kutz" which actually had a pretty good reputation. But this guy honestly drove me insane.

I loved wearing the uniform, but I did need the "high and tight" haircut to seal the deal. I decided to buy into all the hype and give "Kendrix Kutz" a chance. I went to ask him to cut my hair and he laughed and said "Yeah Kendrix Kutz doesn't do those..."

Somehow, despite all the military bases around the world, someone decided Jalen and I both needed to be stationed together in Germany, the exact same base, and the exact same company and platoon. I knew nothing about him other than he refused to give me the much coveted "high and tight," which was all I needed to strongly dislike him.

This guy drove me absolutely insane. He was obnoxious, always making noise, and drawing attention to us. I began to find my groove, and like I mentioned earlier, Stan was doing his part in molding me to become the best I could be. Kendricks and I didn't hang out, and we really didn't talk much more than work required. Then one day we decided to do what's called a "battle drill" which is just executing our plan for this specific scenario just to test everyone's knowledge on said circumstances. I was on day shift, and Kendricks came in for night shift. It was my job to brief him on the exercise which I felt I did a pretty decent job. However, I guess I didn't make it clear that it was a drill. Kendricks dropped his food on the floor, ran to the window, and yelled "Somebody call somebody!" He is a great soldier, don't get me wrong, but finally all his joking around had come back around to him, and for that moment, Kendricks was the focal point of the laughter.

I can't remember the last time I laughed that hard. He was pacing back and forth just picking things up and putting them right back down. It must of been pure chaos in his mind. Finally, one of us was able to stop laughing long enough to get him to calm down. We explained that not only did we complete the drill, but that's all it was - a drill. This was the inside joke for weeks. Years later, Kendricks and I still joke about it, but it served as a key ice breaker between us. The next week we were put on the same shift. We spent our down time getting to know each other a little more, and he even offered to cut my hair. He was willing to give me a high and tight. He admitted he never really knew what it was, and that since he wasn't familiar with what it was, he just told me he didn't do that. He would go on for hours and hours about how when he left the military he was going to own his own barber shop, and I would tell him I was going to own my own gym. This was the link which spawned an incredible friendship.

It used to take him an hour to cut my high and tight, which may have taken the barber shop on post maybe 10 minutes. But it didn't matter. The barber shop was staffed by Germans who didn't speak to you, or at least not in English. Jalen was a perfectionist, and he was passionate. Honestly, the amount of passion he had in what he did I had only seen once before in my life, in my father.

I would be lying if I told you I was some stone-cold soldier who didn't miss home, but once a week Kendricks and I would joke around like my brothers and I did, and he would put every ounce of focus and concentration into cutting my hair, just like my father did with everything he attempted. My father preaches to our team that everything you do matters - every little detail of your life and this was also Jalen's belief. At some point, Kendricks and I started calling each other by first names. Most of you are wondering why I even mentioned that. In the military, your last name is sewn onto your chest, and is called at every roll call. It becomes your only identity. I spent two years overseas and probably don't know the first names of most of the people I saw every day. When Jalen and I started using first names things seemed just a little bit more like home, which was huge for me.

I will admit Jalen had his struggles. He had more potential than he knew what to do with, and sometimes that affected him adversely. He would show up late to PT in the morning, among other little things that allowed him to fall into the shadows.

The Army is pretty simple. Most of the time they tell you exactly where to be, at what time, and even what to bring with you. But if you don't do all those things, you risk being pushed to the back of the line. I saw in Jalen the same thing Stan saw in me. Honestly, I saw in Jalen a lot of myself when I was wasting my life before I joined the military. He was about the same age I was when I was making those mistakes. He joined the military right out of high school. Jalen was strong and athletic beyond measure, but he sold himself short. Jalen needed the same pull that Stan gave me. The reason I say "pull" is because that's what Stan did to me. He didn't get behind me and stop his path to push me forward; he gave me something to strive for. He showed me that the coast was clear ahead, and the fact that he was already in front of me validated that what he was telling me to do and where he was telling me to go, was possible. The best part about wanting to be the best, is when you strive to be the best person you can be, people follow. Not everyone, and normally not a huge number of people, but a select few see you striving for greatness and that's the spark they need to follow in your footsteps. Maybe its competition, maybe it's admiration, but likely it's both. I found this out first hand during my first Army Physical Fitness Test (APFT) in country. Stan, Jalen, and I took a test one morning together. Then it was time for the final event, the two-mile run. My hatred for running is boundless. I dreaded every aspect of it, but it was the only thing keeping me from getting the max score on the PT test. I told myself even if I didn't beat him, I wouldn't lose sight of Stan. I needed a 13 minute or under to max. We all lined up on the starting line right in front of Brigade headquarters. I loved this run route because we were running around the airfield. Since I was a kid, I played with fake military vehicles and G.I. Joe action figures. Now, I was living this dream and running around an airfield filled with Army helicopters calling Army cadences every morning. This feeling was like I was a young kid whose dream was to play in the NFL, and I was walking out for my first game after being drafted. It was that surreal for me each day I woke up on an Army base. I was living my dream.

Get ready, get set, GO! Stan takes of like a jet. Jalen and I are right next to each other like two cars fighting to win the last lap of a NASCAR race. My focus is solely on catching Stan. I began to break away from Jalen a little, and after the first mile, we turned around to head back. I remember feeling like my legs were jello. I had never run this fast, but there was something about chasing Stan that made my legs keep working despite the pain. It was almost over. I glanced back and Jalen is not even in sight. I fly around the final bend and Stan is finished and casually talking to the grader like the run was nothing at all. I felt like I was going to pass out. Who does that? Who runs a 12-minute two-mile and goes straight into a conversation about it?

I cross the finish line and collapse immediately. I closed my eyes, so glad it was over, knowing that even though Stan beat me, at least I beat Jalen by more than a minute. I couldn't make this up, but not two seconds after I collapsed, I thought there was an earthquake. Jalen came flying across the finish line, which by the sound it made, must have been a Superman style leap. He was breathing heavier then I was. We felt like we were dying as Stan just stood their laughing. Stan was ready for another lap.

Jalen may just have wanted to sprint the last straight away, or he may have been chasing me, but for the next two years, I made it a point to give something for Jalen to chase. This had nothing to do with being better than Jalen.

It had everything to do with me being the role model Stan was to me. Jalen and I spent every day together. We fought like brothers, but we excelled together. We fed off each other. We were competitive. The best type of friends are those who can both compete and succeed together.

We spend our whole lives trying to be the best person we can be, best friend, sibling...but I can never truly put into the words the way you feel when you know someone is striving to be like you. It's not about being an "icon" it's about being a role model. I was fortunate enough to be promoted early to Specialist (SPC) on a waiver. Often in our lives we get caught up in our own success, and we lose track of those who helped us get there. I think it's fair to say that sometimes jealousy of other's success gives us a bitter feeling, but not Jalen. When I was selected for promotion, I had every expectation to have tension with my friends. We were all the same rank, and most of them had been eligible longer than I was, including Jalen. Regardless, it was my first promotion in the military, and I had worked very hard. It's not often you see someone like Jalen, who I genuinely believe was even happier about my promotion than I was.

My boss pinned the rank on my chest, and I am not exaggerating when I say that Jalen came running up to congratulate me. He nearly knocked me to the ground with the type of smile I had only seen once before in my life, Papi's. Jalen had his own "unique" laugh, and it caught me off guard to see how genuinely sincere he was. It reminded me of the days when my father told me "You can't do everything in your life alone. It takes teamwork, and a real team shares a heartbeat." That was by definition Jalen. It's tough in the military when you don't have family with you. You miss birthday's, holidays, anniversaries, and when you find success, they are not able to share it with you directly. Jalen made up for all of that: he was my family.

As incredible a feeling my promotion was, I was over-joyed a few months later when Jalen was promoted. I couldn't wait to show him the same pride and excitement he showed me. Our company had set a precedent for when you got promoted. The company would gather, you would read the orders (the official part), and your leadership would say a few words about you and why you deserved this incredible achievement. Regardless of rank, promotion is an incredible accomplishment. What I didn't realize was exactly how much it meant to Jalen. After your leadership speaks, you have the floor. Anytime someone in our com-pany would get promoted and it came time for that person to speak, Jalen would yell from the back of the crowd "Speeeeecccch!" Finally, it was my turn. I had it all planned out. I would take his place yelling "speeeeeech" and as soon as he was done talking, I would be the first to run up and congratulate him. With a tear rolling down his face, the first words out of Jalen's mouth were "I would like to thank my brother Natale." I would be lying if I said I didn't get chills through my body. I missed my brothers so much when I was overseas, and for Jalen to not only call me his brother but called me out to thank me meant the absolute world to me.

He spent his entire opportunity to speak talking about me and his mother. He had told everyone that this was the proudest day of his life, but it wasn't about him. How could a promotion he earned not be about him? So often in our lives when we find success, we celebrate the hard work it took to get there, which is great, but seldom do we take the time to appreciate those who helped guide and support us along the way. Jalen is wise beyond his years. Jalen is the one who convinced me to write this book, and the night of his promotion is the night I decided I would. He told our entire company "no matter what you achieve in life, you can't do it alone, and when you get to where you're going, remember who helped you get there." Those words are the structure of my entire book. Without Jalen, my tour over-seas wouldn't have been the same. Any soldier who tells you they don't miss family when away for that long is likely lying to you. But having friends, indeed a brother, like Jalen, makes all the difference.

Jalen spent Christmas with my family in both 2014 and 2015 and we had the time of our lives. He had heard all the stories I shared about my family, and they heard many about him. I knew that meeting my new brother may help my family sleep a little better when I was away, but more importantly, I wanted Jalen to know what he had done for me would never be forgotten. If Jalen decides to follow his dream and open up his own barber shop, I'll be his first customer. We need people like Jalen to follow their hearts and do what they are truly passionate about. Like my father and Jalen have shown me countless times, passion is what makes the world go 'round.

Mini Me

The night I injured my back may have been one of the scariest moments of my life. We only had one medic with limited supplies, and Ibuprofen can only do so much. My squad leader and I were the only two men to run the entire operations support in the mountains of Slovakia, so despite how severe the injury may be, I was still needed. People still relied on me. I won't lie; when I made it back to my sleeping bag that night, I was in a bit of pain. I rolled over and grabbed my rosary. Every single night since the night before I left for basic I have slept with this red rosary that my Aunt Lulu gave me. I have taken it on every mission, to every country, every night. I grabbed the beads and wove them between my fingers praying the pain would ease, and suddenly my mind was flooded with images of a young man I used to coach. This young man, Casey McCarthy, was on the last team I coached before enlisting. Casey was a living testament to everything my father and I had taught.

Casey's dad had been friends with my father for as long as I can remember. Casey's older brother was in my brother Dom's grade and is also an incredible football player and young man. The McCarthy family never ceases to amaze me. Casey was different from other kids. I had coached a lot of kids, but like I said about Dane (in my father's chapter), you rarely stumble on kids who are both talented and humble. Casey was like a sponge. He willingly soaked in everything you told him and would apply it tenfold. He was the size I was in eighth grade, but there wasn't a person on this planet who could intimidate him. My father would say "he's like a mini you". Mind you I wasn't the best athlete, but I was determined enough to go running into anyone full speed regardless of how far it sent me flying. Casey was much more talented then I was, and he was a much more effective tackler. So, I happily accepted my father's compliment of Casey as my "mini me."

I used to have to ask Casey to dial it back in practice because every time he hit someone, I'd have to drag the victim off the field (and he normally would help) "Sorry coach!" Slowly I successfully distracted from the pain, just thinking about Casey and the memories we shared.

Pain or not, I couldn't help but smile thinking back to the memories of that year. I had created a defensive play we called "letting the dogs off the leash" solely for Casey. It was brilliant. Casey was instructed to do whatever possible to find the guy with the ball and tackle him. Normally, this play ended in pure chaos, but it worked every *time*. Every time I called the play, I looked to my dad and he would say: "Well son, it's up to God how this one ends."

I joke about Casey and his intensity, but it speaks to his passion for the game and for life. And as we've established, passion is essential in every aspect of life. This is why it was beyond tragic when the doctors told Casey he would never play football again. Casey was diagnosed when he was young with a 45-degree curve in his back and a condition where brain tissue expands into the spinal cord. During one of his checkups in high school, he was told the curvature had increased to 68 degrees. His next step would be corrective invasive surgery. Casey endured a 9-hour surgery placing 2 rods and 20 screws into his back to correct the condition. His scar starts at the base of his skull and runs all the way down to his tailbone. He was told he would never be able to play football again. I can't imagine his disappointment. Not only was he incredible at football, but he had poured his heart and soul into the game for years. His passion was potentially taken from him forever. Casey showed me you can try to take something someone is passionate about, but you can't take their passion.

This is why I spoke so highly of Casey and his passion when I coached him, and why we tell all of our players that passion is essential in everything you do, every single time you do it. When you find something you love, don't ever let someone take it from you, fight for what and who you love.

Life never goes the way we plan it to; don't ever put off something today assuming there will be a tomorrow. Indeed, opportunity is like a sunrise, if you wait too long... you will miss it. Casey told his parents if the doctors wouldn't let him play football for fear of him being hit, he was going to be the place kicker for his high school football team. He had never kicked a ball in his life, but that wouldn't stop him. That wouldn't even slow him down. This kid refused to take no for an answer. He was fearless, but more than anything, he was dedicated. The day he shared his plan with me may have been one of the proudest days of my life because Casey took time out of his day to make sure I knew he wasn't quitting. He told me how proud he was to know me. I thought, proud to know me? *I* was proud to know *him*. I could only imagine dealing with what he went through so early in his life.

Casey went to the football field every single day to practice kicking. You can't stop someone who refuses to quit. Every single day, he did exactly what he said he was going to do, and I couldn't be more proud to be a part of his life. So often in our lives we set these goals, or we begin down paths to success and we face setbacks. Casey faced a setback that I bet would cripple most people. His heart and commitment in unprecedented, especially at such a young age. Casey told me "Coach I'm proud to know you; you've helped me through so much." He said something else which sent chills down my spine. He told me he wanted to grow up and be like me and that I was his hero. Any man who claims that wouldn't give him chills is lying. I had a lot of heroes in my life, but this was definitely the first time someone told me I was theirs. The day I was injured isn't the only time I thought of Casey and how he handled a situation with similar circumstances. Thinking of Casey made the pain go away. Fast forward from when I was injured to August when I was home on leave and trying to get my back checked by a specialist. The day I received the MRI results, I was so quick to accept defeat and tell my father my prediction that the Army wouldn't need me anymore. I was very upset because I had worked so hard to get where I was and all of a sudden, the rug was swept right out from under me. I sat in my room and felt pity for myself, until once again, I thought of Casey. This young man faced extreme adversity and struggles so early in his life, and his mindset was incredible and way beyond his years. I won't take credit and say it was because of me or my father. I pray we played a role, but Casey is just an incredible young man with enough drive and motivation to keep the world spinning.

As I sat there feeling sorry for myself, my father and I began to butt heads. He kept reminding me that nothing was certain yet, and there was a chance I could make a full recovery. I was letting my emotions get the best of me, and right before my Dad walked out of the room he asked me what I would tell Casey if Casey came to me with this problem.

I thought back to that day when Casey told me he was picking the football up again, even if it meant as a kicker. Football was still football. I thought about the day he told me he wanted to be like me. How could I be so hypocritical, and not only that...my back injury is nowhere near the severity of Casey's who was half my age. When I texted Casey that night he told me "Coach, it could always be worse, God gave you another opportunity to wake up today". He was so right. The night I was read the MRI results is the day Chris Doyle was killed. That night Casey asked me "what would Chris want you to do now?" Man, that lit a fire under my ass.

This was what I needed to hear. I realized that, being a coach to someone like Casey, I was coaching and growing myself as well. Chris would have wanted me to do what I promised him in basic. I spent all those years with Casey teaching and molding him without realizing I was helping myself too. Coaching is a two-way street. We spend the whole year teaching these young men how to deal with the struggles life brings, how to get back up, how to live your life the way God intended, and how to rely on those around you in moments of both weakness and strength

I sent Casey a message the night before my first surgery. I was just thinking about him, and still being in the Army, there was a chance the problem could be fixed and I could return to full duty. Casey told me the same thing he had told me six months earlier "You just got to keep going coach. It could always be worse." The doctor told me if the surgery was successful, then when I woke up all the pain in my leg would be gone. I was so hopeful. I just wanted to get back to duty. The surgery failed. It helped alleviate some of the pain and my back was still a mess. The Army made the choice that I was officially unfit for duty in May of 2016, and it was a huge blow to the ego. Life really does have a way of testing the words you preach to others. I had really begun to build a name for myself in the Army I planned on having a very successful career. My plans were cut short and my faith was again tested.

Once again, I texted Casey. When I told him I was coming home, the first words out of his mouth were "Does that mean you can come watch me kick this year?" I told him I wouldn't miss it for the world.

It is an amazing feeling when someone looks to you for support, inspiration and motivation. I don't think Casey ever realized how much I admired him. Each time I texted him, he had some good news for me so that I knew he wasn't quitting. First that he was kicking, now he's the starting kicker for Twinsburg High School. The night before I had my second surgery he told me he was going to the Fire Academy to become a fire fighter in the fall. He is unstoppable. I am beyond proud to know Casey McCarthy, and through the toughest transition I've made in my life, he made it a whole lot easier. As nervous as I was to hang up my boots, he reminded me that I would once again prevail. Whatever I end up doing in life, I will do with my whole heart and soul because as much as he said he wants to be like me - I want to be like Casey.

I came home on terminal leave 01 July 2016, and my last official day as a United States soldier was 26 August 2016, exactly three and a half years from the day I left for basic training on 26 February 2013. It was not an easy day for me. I had changed the way I lived my life and fully adapted to military life. I was terrified to re-integrate into civilian life. I never thought any one would tell *me* when my time in the Army was done, and I fought like hell to stay in. God has an incredible way of sending us light in our moments of darkness and that night I received mine. That night was Casey's first football game not only as a senior, but also the starting kicker and captain of his varsity football team at Twinsburg. There was nothing in the world that could keep me from that game, and my father came with me. I rushed to the field so I could be there for the National Anthem and to see Casey charge the field! As I stood with his family by the tunnel his team came running out of, he took my breathe away.

Casey came running out of the tunnel, proudly holding up an American flag flowing in the wind behind him as he led his team to take the field. Tears came flowing down my face. Casey told his coach that he was going to honor me by flying the flag when he took the field, his old coach, on my last day in the Army. He ran it back and forth up and down the sidelines like his own scene from Braveheart. The emotions that ran through me were indescribable. To see him take the field with that flag reminded me that, even though I wasn't in the Army anymore, I had a job to do. I was coaching with my dad again to make an impact in the lives of young men like Casey.

On the kickoff following halftime, Casey made a tackle that shook the stadium. He is by far the most intense and passionate kicker I have ever seen in my life. The tackle he made shook the stadium, and my heart. After everything he went through, his passion continued to grow. I yelled so loud he heard me "Casey!!! YOU ARE MY HERO!" He pointed his finger to his family and me in the stands. You can't take passion away from someone like Casey. It's in his blood and, if he wouldn't let it go neither would I. I may not be a soldier anymore, but I will live my life as if I were, for people like Casey. He is my hero.

Family Away from Home

Arguably, the toughest time I had in the military was when the Army told me I was medically unfit for duty. I began to prepare myself for what seemed to be the inevitable, but it wasn't until the last day I strung up my boots that it sank in. I was a different man before I left for the Army, and I was nervous to go back to the same place and attempt to transition.

So often in our world we hear "things happen for a reason." I guess that saying works, but my father had his own version which applied to my life better: "God puts people in your life for a reason." As tough as the last year of my short career were, there are a group of people who made it manageable. SFC Timothy Cohen, SSG Brian Herriman, and Matt Strickland treated me like family. Let me set the scene and give you just a little background of how I came across these extraordinary gentlemen.

When I was two weeks away from graduating job training, my instructor came up to me and asked if I would be interested in this unit called 160th SOAR. SOAR stands for Special Operations Aviation Regiment and they are the only special operations aviation unit in the Army. All he told me was that I would have to go to "green platoon" which he described as "basic training on steroids." Its purpose being similar to basic training, but to a much more grueling degree, in order to create some of the finest soldiers in the Army and provide beyond excellent aviation support for the United States Special Operations Forces. Before he could even finish the word "operations" in "special operations," I knew I wanted in. But it's not that easy.

I submitted an application packet, and after about a week of sleepless nights, I was informed I got accepted. As excited as I was, I was also informed I would not be leaving. I was previously placed on orders to Germany, and 160th was not able to cancel my overseas orders to take me with them. I was crushed, but for once, I found myself with a different mindset. I had made up my mind that I was going to be a 160th SOAR Nightstalker and was informed all I had to do was reapply after half of my tour was completed, and if accepted, after I completed my tour I would report to green platoon. I worked so hard to be the best soldier I could be overseas. Stan set a two-part goal with me: The first was that I would make it into 160th; the second being I would get promoted to Sergeant (SGT).

Things began to line up for me. My squad leader SGT Ball and I were accepted within a few months of each other. He had been such a huge part of my success in my unit, and he is also the one who sent me to the promotion board. Once I received my promotable status, things were really looking up for me and beginning to line up perfectly. I had fast-tracked to getting my promotable status after a quick 21 months. After Stan passed I pushed myself even harder to fulfill my goals and promises to him. I was all set up to begin green platoon on September 11th, 2015. A few months before I left, SGT Ball and I were a part of a NATO exercise in Slovakia when I hurt my back. When I was cleared by the docs, it was full speed ahead until it was time for me to leave Germany.

This is when I was on leave and was informed just how bad my back injury was. I was in fact, not "cleared" at all; instead, I was looking at a potentially career ending injury. This is also the same time when Chris Doyle was killed. It seemed like in the matter of a few weeks, things went from incredible to absolute chaos. When the doctors at the Cleveland Clinic told me how bad of shape my back was, I knew I wouldn't be starting green platoon. As much as I wanted to be tough, I could barely walk. Injuries heal, but what I was most crushed about was that I had worked so hard to get promoted, and to 160th, and I felt it slipping away. Like I told you in the previous chapter, Casey helped me pick myself up, and the day came when I reported to green platoon.

I reported late on the night of the 26 of August 2015 to hold platoon (where you train and prepare to go to green platoon). I was so nervous. Not because of the training, since I had spent the last year preparing myself for that, but because I had to show up broken. My sciatic nerve was so jacked up I could barely walk, but I had to show up anyway. I had called the NCOIC (the boss) and his name is Sergeant First Class (SFC) Timothy Cohen. I called him about a week before I was supposed to report to inform him of my situation. The night I showed up I was given a temporary room and my only instructions for the morning were to look for SFC Cohen, a tall African American man with a black shirt at 0550. I sat in my bed anticipating what the next day would hold. There must have been 100 soldiers there. I expected to wake up and just be passed off to someone else. There was no way a man who was responsible for that many soldiers would have time to personally attend to some new soldier who showed up "broken." Man, was I wrong.

The reason I put quotes around "broken" is because I was afraid I would show up and he would assume I just didn't want to train. It doesn't look good when you show up to a place like this and the very moment you arrive, you are injured. As much medical documentation as I had, I couldn't help but shake this feeling that I would be "that guy" that everyone thought was faking to escape the hard training. That next morning, I expected to briefly meet SFC Cohen, and after discussing with him my issues he would instruct one of his subordinates attend to me and SFC Cohen would return to the hundreds of other responsibilities someone of his rank and position have. Once again, I was wrong. He dropped everything he had in front of him. Instead of turning the one new problem soldier to one of his cadre, he turned the formation of the other 100 soldiers over.

I had worked so hard to get here, and one thing I longed for the most was this sense of family I heard so much about. Nearly all of the terrific leadership I had in Germany were prior Night Stalkers, and they lived by this incredible code of brotherhood. One of the major reasons green platoon is so important was, upon graduation when you earned your maroon beret, you had earned the right to call yourself a Nightstalker. SFC Cohen didn't know me, I definitely hadn't earned that prestigious title, but he treated me like a son. That first day I showed up he sat with me for six hours so I could get medical attention and medication.

He didn't just pass me off as someone else's problem. Leadership like that is invaluable, because it draws people in. Young soldiers thrive in environments like that because they pull from it. They build from that, and when it's their turn to be in SFC seat years later, they, in turn, treat their soldiers like that. Every workout or training exercise he had them do, he did right by their side. He earned their trust the hard way, but the right way.

That day when SFC Cohen took me to see the docs, he told me he dealt with a similar injury. I soon came to find out he had his fair share of battle wounds. The way he treated me is the way my father had always taught me my entire life is the only way you treat people. You never know what someone is dealing with; you never know what pain someone has. You don't know the life they have, and in the military, you don't know the life they left behind. If you treat people with dignity and respect, show compassion, and most importantly treat them how you want to be treated, looking in the mirror at night becomes easier and easier.

Most soldiers stay at hold platoon anywhere from 1-8 weeks. You work out twice a day, you prepare equipment layouts and inspections, and you have time to get to know the men and women you will have by your side in green platoon when the chaos starts. I spent nearly 11 months there. I worked so hard in Germany to have the highest PT score, and I worked even harder so the day I showed up for green platoon I would physically be ready. I worked so hard in Germany to continue to follow in Stan's footsteps and to be the best I could be in my unit, and I was respected just like he was for my performance and accomplishments. I was used to being the "stud" in Germany when it came to physical fitness and now I could barely walk. That day, SFC Cohen took me to the docs and they told me I wouldn't be training. Actually, the doctor looked me in the eyes and said "Well you know this is probably it for you, right?" Eleven months and I didn't get to train once. I watched class after class go through training. It was so tough to watch other soldiers train for my dream while I was benched.

Roughly a week after my arrival, on 01 September SSG Herriman and Matt Strickland joined the hold platoon cadre. SSG Herriman had been in 160th for well over a decade, and he was coming back as a platoon sergeant to work for SFC Cohen. Matt Strickland had spent a couple years in regiment before he was injured overseas and medically separated. He was coming back as our S1 (performs primary admin duties) and was managing all the incoming soldiers and administrative work reassigning the soldiers who didn't make it. The combination of these three men changed my life. It would have been so easy for any of those three to ship me off to some other unit, but they didn't.

As tough as it was dealing with being on the sidelines I was getting by. Just as I felt I was getting a grasp on my injury, my dad called me and told me Papi wasn't doing well and didn't have much longer. Just three weeks after I arrived at Hold platoon, Papi passed. He had held on for my entire tour overseas. I was crushed because there was no way I could get a leave form signed when I hadn't even been there a month. I was crushed that I thought I would miss his funeral.

Once again, these three incredible men came to the rescue. When I called SSG Herriman to inform him Papi passed, I'll never forget his response: "I'll call you back in two minutes with a signed leave form." I hadn't even asked if I could go home. He decided for me. I was sitting in a pavilion right outside the barracks. He was a man of his word. He told me I could leave that day and I could go home for as long as I needed. SFC Cohen called me too just to tell me how sorry he was to hear my grandfather had passed and to tell me if I needed a ride he would drive me home. I lived eight hours from Ft. Campbell, and this man who barely knew me was willing to drop everything to make sure I made it home for my grandfather's funeral, even if that meant driving me himself in his own truck. Unbelievable. Moments like those are why my dad is spot on when he says people are put in your life for a reason.

After about a month of me doing everything I could to show these men I wanted to stay, SSG Herriman came down and said "Where's my broken guy. I got a job for you." He brought me up to an office and he told me I would be in-processing new soldiers when they arrived. I would help them with their forms and help Matt Strickland manage the soldiers' files. As much as I hated sitting behind a desk, I was ecstatic. Just like Casey saying "football is football," I had a similar mindset. I was still able to wake up every morning and wear the uniform, even if it did take me a little longer to lace up my boots each morning. The Army was still the Army, and I'll take whatever I could get.

I spent the next ten months doing this. These three men went to bat for me to keep me there. They didn't give up and pass me off. If I wasn't at physical therapy or a doctor's appointment, I was there helping them with whatever I could do. I had made up my mind that I would stay there as long as I could until the day came when I could train. Matt and I had become great friends. I began calling him the bearded wonder because he had a righteous beard. In the Army, you have to shave every day. Nearly every soldier dreams of the day as a veteran when the beard can come out of hibernation.

Things were looking good, and I was making some great friends. These three had become like my family away from home. SSG Herriman brought me to his house for Thanksgiving to be with his family. His parents made me dinner on countless occasions and his family treated me like one of their own. As tough a time as this was for me, times like those made it easier.

The doctors had me doing physical therapy, they gave me cortisone injections in my spine, and I had my first surgery in December of 2015. I will never forget the day the three of them sat with me in SFC Cohen's office when he told me "If the docs clear you, we will keep you here for two years if that is what it takes for you to train." I couldn't believe that they had fought so hard to keep someone they barely knew.

The surgery hadn't gone as well as expected. I woke up from the surgery expecting the pain to have receded but it hadn't. I had been walking with a cane at the age of 23. Not exactly how I expected my life to be going. I woke up expecting to be able to walk, but I couldn't. My surgeon told me if this surgery didn't work, there was little chance of me staying in the Army. I was crushed when I woke up because I couldn't fathom having to tell SFC Cohen and SSG Herriman that it didn't work after all they had done for me. I remember the day I returned from recovery leave, and they saw me limping in the door again. Before I even said a word, they knew.

When we sat down, they talked to me about what to expect. We had a pretty good idea this was coming, but that didn't make it easier. My MEB (Medical Evaluation Board) was initiated at the end of January 2016 when I returned. A few months later, the Army came back and said I was unfit for duty, and that was it. All I could think about was I didn't fulfill my promise to Stan. I wouldn't make it into 160th, and I wasn't going to make Sergeant. I remember sitting in barracks room that night holding the SGT rank Stan gave me back on that mission and holding back a fire storm of emotions. As great as it would be to come home and see my family, I couldn't shake the feeling that I had failed both Chris and Stan.

The next day Matt informed me that I would be getting promoted before I was discharged. I don't believe the word exists to accurately describe my excitement and pride. I didn't understand because, right after I received my promotable status, the Army changed the rules. It used to be that if you had enough promotion points, you got promoted. You need a mandatory leadership course, but if you had enough points, you got promoted and you could go to the course when your name came on the list. My unit shut down when I was leaving Germany, and I never went to the course. Even though I had well over 100 more points then I needed to get promoted every month since I passed the board, because I hadn't attended the course, no promotion. Matt told me that, since I was promotable when I was medically separating, the Army would promote me anyway. I couldn't believe it. As crushed as I was to leave the Army, I had fulfilled at least part of my promise to Stan. I was now SGT Timothy A. Natale. Chris would have been so proud.

The last eight weeks before I left, Matt and I became even better friends. He brought his wife to eat with us a few times and brought me into his home to meet his family. My father drove down twice to meet these men who took such good care of me. They gave my dad a unit coin, and I couldn't be happier that he met them. For so long in my life I found much of my father's wisdom hard to grasp. SFC Cohen, SSG Herriman, and Matt Strickland were a living breathing testament to how my father raised me to be. I could not imagine going through that part of my life without them. Every step of the way, they supported me and reminded me that the closing of one chapter of my life was also the opening of another.

I doubt they realize the impact they had on me. Sometimes the littlest pebble can make the biggest splash. SSG Herriman had me over to his house to watch the Super Bowl. This was the first time I could watch the Super Bowl since I had enlisted. I am willing to bet he had no idea that this was Papi and I's favorite time of the year. I watched it with Papi and my father every single year. After Papi died, I dreaded when that time of year came around and he wouldn't be there. SSG Herriman made that night incredible by simply bringing me to watch the game with his family. Matt Strickland invited me to spend a weekend at his house with his wife and daughters so I didn't have to sit in the barracks alone on Mother's Day. I am also willing to bet he didn't know that was the two-year memorial weekend of

Stan's passing. A weekend I spent with Stan and my friends the year before. I had been dreading spending it alone. Matt invited me into his home, and without him knowing, made one of the toughest weekends of the year, enjoyable for me. You never really know how sometimes the simplest acts can do so much to help someone.

When my father came down, he took their families and some of my friends out for a nice steak dinner. These people weren't just leaders to me, they were family. They treated me like their family time and time again. The week before I left, they reminded me it would stay like that forever. SSG Herriman had a going away cookout at his house for me. We just sat around and had the time of our lives. When it was time to leave, they gave me this incredible plaque which I will cherish forever. Never in a million years did I imagine that, when I showed up to Hold platoon, I would be leaving the Army. Beyond that, I never thought I would have made these three great friends. My family has grown tremendously with some incredible people I have met since I enlisted, and Papi had it perfect when he said "family is not determined by blood, but by the way you live your lives and what's in your heart."

Acknowledgements

I still laugh at the fact that I have written a book. I was never the most scholarly, my grammar is terrible, and I would have never thought the day would come where I found myself an author, but here I am. When I was little I looked up to this man who would come into my grade school and talked about writing and all the books he had written. I remember when we would sit on the rug in St. Rita's library and listen to him speak. The way he spoke was incredible. He spoke with so much passion about writing. I couldn't get enough. I loved seeing him in grade school, I was actually really good friends with his daughter Chelsey when we were young. My brother Dominic is great friends with his other daughter Karoline. Both of his daughters went to St. Rita and Notre Dame Cathedral Latin with Dominic and me.

In grade school I used to go home and write these crazy stories for my mom and tell her I was going to be two things when I grew up...a soldier and an author. Never in a million years would I ever think I would have accomplished both of those things, especially the author part. That man that came into my grade school to speak was Mr. Daniel Porter. Not only a very successful author, but such an incredible man to his core. I still have some of the stories I wrote for my mother, they are atrocious to read and I wasn't the best writer but it didn't stop me from doing what I loved. I am a firm believer that you are the only one who controls what you can and can't do in your life. The best skills in life are those which require significant practice.

As I mentioned throughout the book, even when I was at St. Rita I struggled with my life at home, but high school was when it was at its worst. I stopped writing and began my plummet into the darkness where I spent too much of my life. I would see Mr. Porter around NDCL when he was picking up his daughters but I couldn't muster up the courage to go talk to him. I wasn't the same vibrant kid he knew years before. I can't explain it, but every time I saw him I couldn't gain the strength to go talk to the man I had looked up to for so long. Maybe it was because I thought he would look down on the man I had become. My passion for writing never went away, but I never regained the courage and desire to write again until I was overseas. It was my outlet when I got hurt, it was a way for me to relive the memories and to create a way to share those with the world. I wrote parts of this book in every country I have been in. I would write letters to Kelsey Rose when I would lay in my bunk at night, and I would right down the memories I had with my family and friends to keep me from letting the loneliness or fear get the best of me. Stories were all that it was, I had absolutely no idea how to write a book.

When I was home on recovery leave after my first surgery Mr. Porter's daughter Karoline was at my house helping Dominic with some work for his new job. I had to know how her dad was, I hadn't spoken to him in years but I thought about him and his stories all the time. Every single time I wrote, I thought of him. Somehow, I brought up to her that I had thought about writing a book and she suggested I reach out to him. I kept saying I don't know, I hadn't talk to him in years but she insisted. She said "he always asks about you, and how you're doing in the Army." That lit a smile on my face. I couldn't believe he hadn't forgotten about me. I did as she requested and emailed him. A few days later we met at Starbucks in Chagrin Falls and just talked for hours. It was amazing. He was the exact same man as what I remembered. I told him I wanted to write a book and what I wanted it to be about and his smile may have been bigger than mine.

He told me he spoke to so many young kids about writing and I was the only one to ever reach out to him for help with writing a book. Needless to say, he told me that once a month I was to send him whatever I had written and he would help me construct it into a book. He was willing to do whatever I needed to get my book out there, to keep me writing, and write I did. I struggled writing three page papers in high school but a two hundred plus page book was so much different somehow. I wrote this entire book from the true depths of my heart and soul, but I couldn't have done it without his help. You wouldn't be reading this without Mr. Daniel Porter. He believed in me and kept me going. He helped me make my dream come true. He helped me be a man of my word to my mother, I was already a soldier...but now I am an author. When one door closes another opens. I can't thank him enough for what he has done for me. I owe him the world. He is like family to me now, and he is my hero.

There are not enough pages to thank him for what he has done for me, or to acknowledge everyone who has made an impact on my life. This book was difficult to write because eventually I had to stop writing. There are so many more chapters to write, so many more experiences to tell, to many more people to thank but this is it for now. Thank you to everyone who believed in me, when I didn't believe in myself. Mr. Porter and his entire family for their help with my journey to becoming an author.

Life is the ultimate team sport and it took me a very long time to figure that out, but I did and I hope through this book I was able to share that with you. I would like to thank all of my fellow soldiers and military members who are still fighting for our country. I thank those men and women who paid the ultimate sacrifice so I could continue to live my life and continue to do things like write this book. You will always be in my prayers, there's not a day that goes by that I don't wish I could be right by your side again. I will live my life to make your sacrifice worth it. Lastly, I would like to thank the St. Rita football teams and families; past, present, and future. It's much more than just football, our team is another family to my father and I. Before I joined the Army, you were my pride and joy. It started with me just coaching to spend time with my father, but I grew to adore every minute God gave me on the field teaching and growing with all of you. When I left the Army, I was lost, I didn't know what to do if I couldn't be a soldier anymore. Well I'm here to tell you coaching you all is what I am meant to do. You have given my father and I serenity and pride like you will never know. You gave me purpose when I was lost. I promised God if I made it home to step foot on the field again with you, I would be the best coach I could possibly be. I promised to offer my heart and soul up to that team year after year, and I will keep that promise. Thank you and I will continue to live Chris Doyle and Stan's legacy on through you.

The Bridge

It just wouldn't be right to call this last part a "conclusion." In fact, if I had to call it that, it might give off the impression that I am content with the man in the mirror, and this is the end of my journey. It's not, and my journey in life has just begun. I have been beyond blessed with the people I have met throughout my life so far, and it took me a long time to realize that. So often in my life I've wondered why I am where I am and why I do what I do. I don't mean just in the military, even though that has been a huge portion, but in everyday life. The military has thrown some tough times at me, and so has life in general. These stories I have shared with you are my reminders for why I strive to be the best person I can be. These memories play in my head on repeat every single day. Each person has a huge part in my continued growth and the man I am, each person is a part of my man in the mirror. No one is perfect, and there will never be a day when I look in the mirror and am content with who I am. I will continue to grow and build the man in the mirror. Everyone has good and bad experiences in life, will meet good and bad people, but the combination of those experiences and people make us who we are. Just like a young kid may swing the baseball bat like his favorite player, that mentality of adapting our hero's characteristics, traits, and experiences are what make us unique. Live your life to be someone else's hero.

Every night when I look myself in the mirror, I can smile regardless of how tough my day has been. I still have my fair share of flaws and shortcomings, but that is the reason why my father told me to look in the mirror in the morning *and* at night. When we wake up in the morning, we set goals; we decide how we are going to live that day; we decide who we are going to be that day. When we look in the mirror at night, we hold ourselves accountable. Did I do what I said I was going to do; did I act the way I wanted to act; did I reach my goals or at least take a step in the right direction; did I treat people the way I was taught to treat people; and was I the best I could be? As tough as criticism is, it doesn't have to be negative. Like I said in the beginning, I looked in the mirror through pure negativity, anger, and frustration for so long. That's not what life is about. Be proud of who you are, realize it's never too late to change, and work to make yourself and others around you better every day. At the end of the day, if you aren't happy with who you see in that mirror, when you wake up the next day, picture who you want to be, and work towards being that person.

So often in our lives, especially as the years progress, we hit rough patches where we wonder if the next day we wake up will be the start of another battle. If the next morning will be the last day of struggle or the start of the climb back on top. I spent years of my life in what felt like my own rock bottom. I begged for the day when things started to change, when I would be proud of myself and the man in the mirror, and when I finally fell asleep excited to wake up the next morning. It wasn't until I noticed what and who was still around me in at the bottom that I noticed it was up to me to crawl back up the hill. It was the hardest thing I have done so far in my life. I completely changed the way I see the world, but I didn't do it alone. When the day comes that you find yourself at the "top" of the hill, be proud. Stay humble, and take a look around you at all those people who helped to lift you up there, with a smile on their face.

I may still be fighting that old battle if I hadn't realized all the people around me who were fighting with me and for me. You can't go through life alone; even Jesus had followers to help him spread the word. Teamwork is necessary for success. Even on my best days I still strive to make myself better. I want to change the world, and it starts with me. I had to learn to approach life one day at a time, before I could go out and make the world a better place, I needed to make myself better. Family and friends are irreplaceable. There is no value on true friendship. There is no telling where I would be without these people in my life. The success I found in the military is because of the support I had and the people who believed in me. The people who held me up when I felt weak. Now it's my turn to hold the world up just like that, one person at a time.

As I said before, as nervous as I was the join the Army, I was more nervous to come home. Nobody likes being told "you can't do this anymore" especially when I was so young. Two back surgeries by the age of twenty-four and there are days when I can't put my own socks on, but at least I have socks. There are days I don't walk very well, but I can still walk. There are days I can't stand so well, but I still stand. I never thought I would ever need a cane at this age, even if it was temporary. Life doesn't go how we plan it, but that's ok...it can always be worse. No matter how tough you think your life is, there is always someone out there who has it worse. No matter how hard life knocks me down, I will ALWAYS get back up and fight back because I have people to stand and fight for. Everyone has their reasons to get back up, whether it's someone who relies on you or something internal...there is always a reason to get back up and keep fighting, always.

As scary as the reintegration to civilian life would be, I knew I would survive. I had grown so much since I left, but more importantly, my desire to continue to grow as a man is even stronger. I kept telling myself "wherever life takes me, I'll survive" but I was wrong. It's not about where life takes me but it's about where *I* take *life* that will ensure my success. I promised Chris and Stan before God called them home that we would change the world and leave a legacy, and that promise stands true. I am where I am because of the people who helped me along the way. I hope you can be one of those people, too, and that you thank those who help you along the way.

Made in the USA
Columbia, SC
10 September 2018